Pendeen Watch lighthouse is one link in a chain of navigation aids helping mariners navigate Cornwall's treacherous coasts. NICHOLAS LEACH

THE NATURE OF CORNWALL'S COASTLINE

Cornwall's long coastline presents many dangers to the mariner who is either navigating past it on to other destinations or intending to enter one of its ports or harbours. Along the south coast are many inlets, wide bays, estuaries and natural harbours, which can safely accommodate vessels both small and large but whose entrances can often catch out the unwary navigator. The north coast, on the other hand, is characterised by rugged cliffs and rocks which take the full force of the Atlantic ocean in the prevailing westerly wind, which frequently rises to gale force during the winter months.

Many vessels have been wrecked on the coast of Cornwall, which has a reputation for being one of the most treacherous in Britain. One of the earliest recorded disasters occurred in January 1814 when the transport ship *Queen*, which had anchored off Falmouth, was wrecked. In a violent south-easterly storm, the ship's anchor cable parted and she was blown onto the rocks of Trefusis Point. More than 300 people were on board of whom fewer than 100 survived, mainly by swimming ashore.

Industrialisation in the eighteenth and nineteenth centuries resulted in an increasing number of ships involved in Britain's expanding coastal and foreign trades. More ships at sea inevitably led to a higher incidence of wrecks. Concern about ship losses mounted between the 1770s and the 1800s, and the need for some form of boat on shore ready to put out to save vessels in distress became acute.

As trading ships were at the mercy of storms and gales, shipwreck meant the loss of valuable crews and cargoes. Many vessels were stranded or wrecked through factors beyond the control of those on board or otherwise involved with the ship, which could easily be caught in bad weather with nowhere to shelter. Navigating also presented many hazards. Passing through shoals, near rocks or around sandbanks was often fraught with difficulties.

At night, navigation was even more difficult. Lighthouses were needed at the most dangerous points on the coast, as were leading lights to guide ships into ports. As early as the sixteenth century there is evidence of lights being displayed to help guide the mariner in Cornwall. The major hazards offshore, such as the Wolf Rock, have since been marked by lighthouses, as have the most dangerous headlands, such as Trevose Head near Padstow. Today, more lighthouses can be found on the Cornish coast than in any other county in Britain – as described in the companion volume *Cornwall's Lighthouse Heritage*.

Before any means to save lives from vessels in distress had been established, locals would often attend a wreck only with the intention of plundering the cargo and anything else they could gain from it, such as timber from the vessel's hull. This practice, known as wrecking, was quite widespread throughout the county, which has gained the reputation for having some of the most notorious wreckers, particularly during the eighteenth century. There are tales that false lights were exhibited to lure vessels onto the shore to plunder the cargo and even murder the survivors. However, during the early years of the nineteenth century the practice gradually ceased as customs and coastguard officers became more efficient at enforcing the laws against such actions.

Before lifeboats were operated, rescues were performed by local people often using their own boats. At many of Cornwall's ports, the light, narrow boats built for speed, known as gigs, were employed as work boats by local seamen for all kinds of tasks. They were often used by coastguards or pilots to go to wrecks, particularly on the Isles of Scilly where many rescues were effected using them. In February 1830, they were used to save twenty-one people from the *Borodino*, which had been driven onto rocks. In 1838, the schooner *Victoria*, of Exeter, was wrecked in Crow Sound, and three gigs were used to save her crew of six. Some of the rescuers received awards from a variety of bodies, including the National Institution, which recognised both lifeboat crews and anyone else who had rescued lives from shipwreck.

THE FIRST LIFEBOATS IN CORNWALL

It is difficult to establish with certainty when and where life-saving at sea began. The first attempts to place lifeboats on Britain's coast were made during the last quarter of the eighteenth century, a time when the nation's industrial growth was gathering momentum. The first recorded lifeboat on the west coast was placed at Formby in the mid-1770s, set up and financed by the Docks Commissioners at Liverpool, a port that was expanding rapidly due largely to the insidious slave trade as well as industrial advances. On the east coast, the fastest growing port was Newcastle, which was heavily involved in the coastal trade to London. It is no surprise, therefore, that the first boat designed and built specifically for life-saving has its origins in the city. It was built by Henry Greathead in 1790 at South Shields, on the south bank of the mouth of the river Tyne, and operated from there for several decades. Therefore, as the foundations of industry were laid between the 1770s and the 1820s, so were the foundations of Britain's lifeboat service.

The shipowners' and underwriters' growing awareness of ship losses prompted greater efforts on their part to reduce dangers to life, ships and trade, particularly on the east coast of England, along which most of Britain's coastal trade was carried. During the first decade of the nineteenth century, Lloyd's insurance agency, in London, set up a fund which promoted the building and operating of lifeboats to counter ship losses, and ports were encouraged to operate their own lifeboat. This fund provided an impetus to early lifeboat building and helped pay for, amongst others, Cornwall's first lifeboat which was stationed at Penzance in 1803.

The Penzance boat was one of more than thirty boats built by Greathead based on the lifeboat he built for South Shields in 1790, the success of which led to the design being adopted upon which most early lifeboats were based. The boat built for Penzance was 27ft by 10ft in size and cost 150 guineas, of which Lloyds contributed £50, while the remainder was made up by locally raised subscriptions. The initial enthusiasm for the project is reflected by the long list of subscribers that was published in the *Royal Cornwall Gazette* of 29 October 1803.

Although this lifeboat was kept serviceable during the first few years of her existence, she was in fact never used for life-saving. On 22 October 1805, when Cornwall was visited by 'a most tremendous gale', she is stated to have been 'kept in a state of readiness in case of accident' but was not called upon. Several vessels sheltered at Penzance during this storm, but the lifeboat was not called upon to assist any of them. Nothing more is known of this lifeboat until 1812, when she was

LIFE BOAT.

Drawing of a Greathead-built lifeboat, similar to that used at Penzance and partly funded by Lloyds

sold for 20 guineas, never having been used. Despite the pioneering efforts to secure a lifeboat for Penzance, interest in the project had waned to such an extent that she was disposed of.

The reason for the relative failure of this first lifeboat is a matter of conjecture. Although there was not a great demand for such a boat in the relatively quiet trading routes around west Cornwall, the natural hazards of Mount's Bay were enough to justify its existence. However, the poverty of the county in general would have probably meant that monies needed for its upkeep and operation were scant; indeed, this is supported by a statement made in the *West Briton* newspaper at the time of the lifeboat's sale. It said: 'Perhaps the Gentlemen of Penzance and its neighbourhood feel themselves so burthened by providing the poor with provisions . . . that they have nothing to spare for redeeming the Life-boat.'

LOCAL INITIATIVES TO PROVIDE LIFEBOATS

Before a national lifeboat organisation had been founded, local individuals and bodies took responsibility for funding and managing lifeboats where they were deemed necessary. Lifeboats were established at those places where vessels were most often at risk and where a crew could readily be obtained. This was often at, or relatively close to, a harbour such as that at Padstow, formed by the estuary of the river Camel. Offering a natural haven for ships, the port was used by a great variety and number of vessels. However, it had a treacherous entrance through which it was difficult to navigate. Many vessels were lost at the entrance to the estuary, where the aptly named Doom Bar and Hell Bay caught out vessels entering the harbour in a westerly gale. The dangers of the harbour entrance suggested the need for a lifeboat at the port.

The first Padstow lifeboat was provided in 1827, built locally by Tredwen at a cost of £50, and was only 23ft in length. This boat was supposedly named *Mariner's Friend*, and was probably kept at first on the Quay. She had been paid for by a collection made locally, to which the National Institution contributed £10. In November 1829, the Padstow

The small self-righting lifeboat ARAB (ON.51) being hauled out of the lifeboat house at Hawker's Cove. The small building on the left was used as a boathouse for the station's first lifeboat in the 1820s.

Harbour Association was founded and one its aims was 'to provide accommodation for the lifeboat and Manby's Mortar Apparatus' that were already in operation at the port. The lifeboat was thus placed under their authority. It was then moved to Hawker's Cove, a small sheltered inlet nearer the mouth of the estuary from where it could be launched more easily. The list of subscriptions made to the Association in 1830 was headed by companies and commercial concerns, notably the Merchant Venturers Society of Bristol and Messrs Vivian and Sons, a Swansea company, together with many other companies and private individuals. Clearly commercial trading concerns could see the benefit of a lifeboat to their own operations.

Between 1803 and the founding of National Institution in 1824, no more lifeboats were built for service in Cornwall, although at Bude on the north coast records suggest that the Admiralty provided a boat in 1817. Although details of such a boat, if it existed, are patchy, in 1837 a local committee did succeed in establishing a lifeboat after two vessels were wrecked off Bude during a storm on 29 October 1836. The incident was brought to the attention of the King, William IV, by the Reverend Ellacoat, a local resident. The monarch then 'most promptly and munificently commanded that a sum of money should be given from the Duke of Cornwall for the purpose of establishing a lifeboat at Bude'.

The lifeboat built for Bude was of a design similar to Greathead's lifeboats which, although popular in its native north-east, was disliked elsewhere and Bude was no exception. When the boat capsized in October 1844 with the loss of two men during a practice launch, any confidence which the crew had in it evaporated. This accident furthered the local boatmen's dislike for the boat and lead to its eventual demise. By the early 1850s it had been neglected and was in poor repair.

At St Ives, another independently funded lifeboat was operated, unusual to the county in that it was designed locally. The impetus to build a lifeboat came about as a result of two events: a wreck within sight of the port, and a competition organised by the Royal Cornwall Polytechnic Society. On 24 December 1838, in a heavy gale, the schooner

Rival grounded on one of St Ives' harbour piers. Local pilots using gigs attempted a rescue; others tried Manby's mortar apparatus; and a fishing boat was also launched, but all to no avail. Later the same day, the pilots went out again in one of the fishing boats and after showing much courage and expending great effort they succeeded in saving five from the schooner. At the meeting held to make monetary rewards to those involved in this rescue, a discussion took place on 'the expediency of providing a lifeboat for this port'. Fortunately for all those at the meeting, building a lifeboat for the port was distinctly feasible thanks to the foresightedness of the Royal Cornwall Polytechnic Society.

In 1838, this Society held a competition seeking the best model of a lifeboat. At this time, all kinds of fanciful suggestions for and designs of rescue boats were being put forward in both the local and national press, most totally impractical. However, the winning design, by Francis Adams, was neither fanciful nor impractical. Adams, a St Ives boatbuilder, designed his boat with two objectives in mind: first, that it should be highly manoeuvrable when near a wreck, and second, that it should be unsinkable under all circumstances – a somewhat optimistic if laudable aim. To attain the first aim his model had two bows so that, both ends being alike, she could be rowed in either direction without the boat itself being turned round. The rowers effected the change of direction by turning round and facing themselves in the opposite direction. As well as this novel principle of steering, she was clinker built, contained air-tight vessels at each end to provide extra buoyancy, and was fitted up like the local gigs.

The combination of a readily available lifeboat design with the need for a lifeboat (evident from the *Rival* wreck) led to the proposal for a lifeboat for St Ives becoming a reality. The favourable reception gained by Adams' design led to the new boat being built by the designer himself. It was constructed in

The 37ft self-righting lifeboat Bob Newbon (ON.371) which served at Falmouth from October 1894 to August 1922 with Coxswain Samuel Hingston at the stern.

CHRONOLOGY: EARLY LIFEBOATS IN CORNWALL

1790 Greathead builds first lifeboat in South Shields, 30ft in length and pulled by ten oars, had a curved keel and a double ended hull.

1803 First lifeboat in Cornwall at Penzance, built by Greathead, and in operation until 1812 but never used.

1826 Attempts to revive the Penzance station by the RNIPLS.

1827 A small four-oared lifeboat was built locally at Padstow and served there until the 1850s. It was a non-self-righting vessel and, in 1829, came under the auspices of the newly-formed Padstow Harbour Association.

1837 Lifeboat provided for Bude, 24ft 9in in length and built by Wake of Sunderland, was known as the Royal Bude Lifeboat.

1837 First lifeboat sent to the Isles of Scilly, an 1825-built six-oared craft designed and built by William Plenty of Newbury.

1840 A lifeboat was built locally by Francis Adams for service at St Ives. Funded by local subscriptions, the small six-oared boat cost £120 and was reputedly named *Hope*.

1853 The National Institution established a lifeboat station at Sennen Cove and went on to found a series of new stations in Cornwall.

accordance with the proposals laid down in his model and was 30ft in length. Being locally designed and built the new lifeboat was looked upon most favourably by the local boatmen who were to man her. A subscription fund to pay for the new boat organised by the local MP, Mr W. T. Praed, was well supported by many local people.

The new lifeboat, named *Hope*, was inaugurated at a well-attended ceremony on 11 January 1840 when she went to sea for a demonstration run under the command of Mr Martin, Chief Officer of the local Coastguard. During her career, she was kept in a fish cellar adjoining the coastguard boathouse on the beach, and is known to have performed at least one service, on 7 April 1840, when she went to the smack *Mary Ann*, of Poole which went ashore during a heavy gale. The lifeboat made two fruitless attempts to reach the vessel and, filled with water, was thrown onto the beach by the strength of the seas. Eventually two men risked their lives by swimming to the smack and saving those on board it.

A NATIONAL ORGANISATION

In 1823, Sir William Hillary, of Douglas in the Isle of Man, wrote and published 'An Appeal to the British Nation on the Humanity and Policy of forming a National Institution for the Preservation of Lives and Property from Shipwreck'. In this he set out his ideas for the formation of a national body whose sole responsibility would be the preservation of human life from shipwreck. Largely as a result of the exertions of Sir William, the Royal National Institution for the Preservation of Life from Shipwreck (RNIPLS) was founded at a meeting in London on 4 March 1824.

Initially, the newly-formed National Institution was quite successful in fulfilling its aims, and added to the number of lifeboats in operation. One of its earliest ventures was the re-establishment of a lifeboat at Penzance in 1826 when a small 24ft lifeboat, built by William Plenty of Newbury, was supplied. Unfortunately, the boat lasted only two years for reasons that have not been recorded but again lack of funds and local support probably account for its short life. The Institution also gave funds to the organisers behind the lifeboat built for Padstow in 1827.

The first Porthoustock lifeboat MARY ANN STORY, a 33ft self-righter built by Woolfe at Shadwell, was typical of the lifeboats that saw service throughout Cornwall during the latter half of the nineteenth century. She served the station from 1869 until 1886 and is credited with saving 43 lives. RNLI

The 32ft self-righter RICHARD LEWIS at Penzance where she was stationed from 1865 to 1884. This photo, dating from about 1868, was taken outside the lifeboat house built at the western end of Penzance promenade in 1856. In December 1868 she capsized on service without loss of life. RNLI

Another station established with the assistance of the embryonic National Institution was at St Mary's in the Isles of Scilly, where wrecks were frequent because of the nature of the coastline. In 1837, the Inspecting Commander of Coastguard on the Isles of Scilly, Captain Charles Steel, collected money for a lifeboat to operate in the islands. He wrote to the National Institution and sent the £26.19s.6d that he had collected. At a meeting of the Committee of Management on 21 June 1837, it was agreed to transfer the former Brighton lifeboat, built in 1824 but never used for life-saving, to the Isles of Scilly. The boat arrived in September 1837 and a boathouse was built for it on the beach at Hugh Town, St Mary's, where a crew could always be obtained. However, at 20ft by 6ft 9in, the boat was too small and not liked by its crew. After only two years at St Mary's, having never been used on service, it was condemned and broken up.

Following this first somewhat unsuccessful attempt to operate a lifeboat at St Mary's, Captain Steel requested a larger lifeboat from the Institution. They complied by sending a boat which, like its predecessor, had also been built by William Plenty, but was 26ft by 8ft 6in, rowing ten oars rather than six. Previously stationed at Plymouth, it had never been used there. At St Mary's, it was only used once, in January 1841, when it went to the aid of the steam packet *Thames*, on passage from Dublin to London, which had been wrecked on the Western Rocks in a severe gale. Despite the best efforts of Captain Steel and the volunteers who manned the boat, together with other local gigs, the steam packet broke up with the loss of fifty-seven lives. Only one person survived, and eight bodies were recovered by the lifeboat. For his gallantry on this occasion, the Gold medal of the National Institution was awarded to Captain Steel and Silver medals to four of the Coastguard men that accompanied him in the lifeboat.

In view of this tragedy, improvements were needed to make the lifeboat at St Mary's more effective, yet nothing was done. The seas around the islands, which formed an important shipping lane, were both busy and treacherous and a lifeboat was clearly needed. The failure to improve matters can be attributed to the scarcity of funds available to the National Institution and the lack of a suitably powerful lifeboat design. The small lifeboats of the pre-1850 era, which were generally under 30ft in length and relied solely on manpower, were totally inadequate in the face of the seas off Scilly. Reaching wrecks on the outer islands in such a craft would have been almost impossible in bad weather. But whatever the reasons, nothing more is known of this second lifeboat until 1855 when it was removed.

Considering the treacherous nature of the Cornish coastline, it is surprising that more lifeboats were not built for the county during the early years of the nineteenth century. But the finance necessary to operate and maintain lifeboats was not readily available locally, unlike at major ports such as Newcastle and Liverpool. The county was relatively poor and money for sea rescue was only forthcoming intermittently. The inherent dangers of the Cornish coast, and increasing numbers of vessels passing the county due to the growth of trade, seem to have had little impact on lifeboat operation as none of the early Cornish lifeboats were particularly successful.

Launch of the Mevagissey lifeboat JOHN ARTHUR (ON.224) from the boathouse built in the outer harbour in 1895-6. This 37ft self-righter served the station from 1888 to 1895 and saved two lives.

The National Shipwreck Institution, as the RNIPLS became known, helped the situation in the years immediately after its founding, but by the 1830s faltered through lack of funds. Since its inception in 1824, raising money for lifeboats had proved difficult, and annual income dwindled during the 1830s and 1840s. By 1850, with no public appeals made for over a decade, the level of finance available to the Committee of Management was at its lowest level. Reform was essential if the Institution was to continue its work.

Matters came to a head following a disaster at the mouth of the river Tyne in December 1849 when one of the local lifeboats capsized in sight of the land with the loss of twenty out of twenty-four on board. This event highlighted the need for more efficient lifeboats, that could perform the task of saving life at sea effectively. Soon after, there was an upturn in the fortunes of the RNIPLS when Richard Lewis and the Duke of Northumberland, then First Lord of the Admiralty, became the Institution's Secretary and President respectively. These two men were to have a considerable impact on the Institution during the next few decades. It was evident to both that reform was urgently needed, and during the early 1850s, under their guidance first reforms were implemented. The service was re-organised and renamed the Royal National Lifeboat Institution (RNLI), and throughout the rest of the century became increasingly efficient.

The Duke of Northumberland soon realised that not only was reform of the Institution necessary but a new design of lifeboat was also essential. After consulting with the Institution's Chairman and Deputy Chairman in May 1850, the Duke drew up a prospectus for a national competition to

Lizard lifeboat ADMIRAL SIR GEORGE BACK (ON.509) attending the wreck of the ship HANSY, of Fredrikstad in November 1911.

Launch of the Bude lifeboat Elizabeth Moore Garden *(ON.52), a 34ft standard self-righter which was on station from 1886 to 1911. Bude was one of many stations established in Cornwall by the RNLI during the second half of the nineteenth century.*

test the ideas of boatbuilders and designers throughout the nation. Out of 282 plans submitted, the design of the Great Yarmouth boatbuilder, James Beeching, was the eventual winner. His boat employed a principle of self-righting achieved by a low waist and high air-cases at each end, causing the boat to come upright in the event of a capsize. Beeching built several boats to his design, which was subsequently modified and improved by James Peake, Master Shipwright of the Royal Naval Dockyard at Woolwich, under the instructions of the Institution. The Peake designed self-righter was altered and improved over time, and eventually the self-righter became the accepted type throughout the country, apart from in Norfolk and Suffolk.

With a new design of lifeboat available and the newly renamed Institution on a relatively sound financial footing, the Committee of Management embarked on a fairly rapid programme of boat building, and established many new stations throughout the country. The first new station to be established in Cornwall during this expansion was at Sennen Cove, a small hamlet about a mile north of Land's End. A lifeboat was placed here as the direct result of a shipwreck that occurred in November 1851 which, as well as drawing attention to the need for a lifeboat in the area, also resulted in one of the most heroic rescues ever undertaken in Cornwall being performed.

Early in the morning of 11 November 1851 in thick fog the brig *New Commercial*, of Whitby, struck the Brisons, a pair of rocks off Cape Cornwall, and broke up immediately. The crew of nine, together with the master's wife, reached a ledge on the rock from where they were seen at daybreak, but because of the seas running very high nothing could be done to assist them. At 9am, a large wave washed them off the ledge, and all but three drowned. One managed to leave the rock on a portion of floating wreck, and was picked up by a small boat that had been launched by the Sennen fishermen. The other two, the master and his wife, remained on the Little Brison. Throughout the afternoon of the 11th further attempts were made to reach them but nobody could despite the revenue cutter *Sylvia* coming from Penzance to assist.

By the following morning, hundreds of people thronged the cliffs to watch no fewer than six vessels, variously manned by coastguards and fishermen, attempt to approach the rock and effect a rescue but the sea was so high that no boat could venture to within 100 yards of the rock. However, Captain George Davies, Inspecting Commander of the Coastguard at Penzance, who was in one of the boats on the scene, had taken with him a nine-pound rocket. Although this rocket had never been tried here before, either on land or in a boat, it was the only chance to successfully rescue the two survivors on the rock, who were by now in a terrible condition. The danger to Davies of firing the rocket from his boat, with a line attached, was considerable but he decided it was the best hope for the two survivors.

The first line that was fired fell short into the sea, but the second reached the rock and landed close to the master. His wife then jumped into the sea with the line attached, and was pulled to the boat but unfortunately died of exhaustion before reaching the shore. The master was pulled into another boat, after which all were safely landed at Sennen. For the outstanding effort made in trying to effect a rescue throughout the two days, Captain Davies, who became Inspector of Lifeboats soon afterwards, and Thomas Randall,

The lifeboat ELIZABETH AND BLANCHE (ON.424) under the cliff at Newlyn, from where she was operated between 1908 and 1913. In 1913 she was transferred to Penlee to become the first lifeboat to launch from the boathouse at Penlee Point. In this photo, dating from about 1911, some of the crew are wearing cork lifejackets and some kapok.

Commander of the cutter *Sylvia*, were both awarded the RNLI's Gold medal; Silver medals went to various other coastguard men; and other awards were made to the Sennen boatmen who had put out in the atrocious conditions to help.

Following this notable wreck and rescue, steps were taken to establish a lifeboat station at Sennen. At the Annual General meeting of the RNLI held on 22 April 1852, it was reported that a boat was ready to be sent to Sennen, 'in acknowledgement of the gallant conduct of the Coast Guards and fishermen of that place on the occasion of the wreck of the ship *New Commercial* on the Brisons'. The new boat was a small, light self-righter, to James Peake's design, 25ft 8in in length, 6ft 10in in breadth, and rowing six oars. This boat served at Sennen until 1864, performing only one service, on 6-7 May 1856, when she assisted the barque *Charles Adolphe* into Penzance.

In addition to the new station at Sennen, further new lifeboats were built for Bude, Penzance (both in 1853) and Padstow (in 1856), where lifeboats had been placed before. As the financial position of the RNLI improved during the 1850s, the Institution was able to examine the extent of the lifeboat coverage on Cornwall's coast. Not only were new lifeboats provided for the stations already mentioned, but completely new places were provided with lifeboats to cover various danger spots. Between 1859 and 1863 four additional stations were established: Polkerris and Lizard (both in 1859), Newquay (in 1860) and Porthleven (in 1863), bringing to eight the number of lifeboats in Cornwall. Within a decade of the Institution being reformed, the most dangerous hazards off the county's coastline had been covered.

The new stations at Polkerris and Lizard were of particular significance as they were the first lifeboats on Cornwall's south coast. Hitherto, no lifeboat was in operation between Penzance to the west and Teignmouth, in Devon, to the east. Polkerris is a small village at the eastern end of St Austell Bay, in which the two small harbours of Charlestown and Pentewan are situated. Since the 1820s, these harbours attracted an increasing number of vessels mainly involved with the china-clay industry. In 1832, to assist vessels navigate a passage an 84ft high red and white striped landmark was built on Gribbin Head, at the eastern tip of the Bay. Despite this, however, the schooner *Endeavour*, of Ipswich, was wrecked off Gribbin Head on 6 May 1856 after she had been driven ashore by a gale in Polkerris Bay.

The coastguard attempted to reach the schooner but failed due to the severe weather conditions. Those on the scene sent for a small boat and ropes which were duly sent from Polkerris. This small boat, a punt, was lowered down the cliffs, followed by three men who manned her. With a large crowd of onlookers, and after a great struggle in the ferocious conditions, the punt was manoeuvred towards the only survivor who was successfully rescued and brought ashore.

Following these events, William Rashleigh, the local landowner, wrote to the RNLI requesting a lifeboat for the area. Selecting the best site for the station proved difficult as, although Fowey was deemed the most suitable location with its large resident population, the harbour entrance would not be navigable to a pulling and sailing lifeboat during onshore gales when she was most likely to be needed. The matter was left for three years until further pressure from Rashleigh, who also contributed money and material for the building of a lifeboat house, and other local gentry resulted in Polkerris being chosen as the most suitable site as it offered a sheltered launching area. A lifeboat house was built on the beach and a 30ft six-oared self-righting lifeboat named *Catherine Rashleigh* supplied.

As with Sennen in 1851 and Polkerris in 1856, the establishment of a lifeboat station at the Lizard also came about following a tragic accident in the area. On 22 January 1859, the steamship *Czar* struck the Vrogue Rock and within half an hour had sunk. Those on board tried to get away, and while some succeeded and some were rescued by the coastguard, thirteen others lost their lives. This event was brought to the attention of T. J. Agar Robartes, of Lanhydrock, a landowner in the county, who ascertained the practicality of having a lifeboat stationed at or near the Lizard.

A debate about the best site for a lifeboat station on the Lizard ensued. Some believed Mullion to the west was the most suitable location but local opinion favoured Polpeor Cove, at the southern tip of the Lizard, which was centrally placed so a lifeboat could most easily reach to either side of the peninsula. Agar Robartes then contacted the Institution saying that he and his mother would fund the cost of establishing the station, providing both lifeboat and boathouse. The Institution immediately accepted this offer; a

Hayle lifeboat ADMIRAL RODD *(ON.567), a 36ft self-righter, with officials, crew and helpers, probably on the day of her arrival at the station in December 1906. She served until 1920, when the station was closed.*
ROYAL INSTITUTION OF CORNWALL

boathouse was built and in November 1859 the new lifeboat, a 30ft six-oared self-righter named *Anna Maria*, arrived. The total cost of the new lifeboat station was £269. In spite of the fine intentions of Agar Robartes in getting the Lizard station established, its first lifeboat met with a tragic end. During a routine exercise on 2 January 1866, she was wrecked with the loss of three lifeboatmen. She was quickly replaced by another boat of similar size and design.

By the time Lizard's second lifeboat had been placed on station, frequent wrecks had made it clear that further lifeboat stations were needed to cover the east and west of the Lizard peninsula. New stations were therefore opened in 1867 at Mullion on the western side and Cadgwith on the eastern side. Both places afforded sheltered launching sites and could provide an adequate number of men to form a crew. Both stations received the larger 33ft self-righting lifeboat, which was ten oared, and was more capable than the smaller 30ft version at the Lizard.

The success of the RNLI in establishing lifeboat stations after the reforms of the 1850s was down to a combination of factors. Internal reorganisation, the introduction of *The Lifeboat* journal in 1851 and the Charter of Incorporation authorised by Queen Victoria in 1860 all increased public awareness of the Institution and its work, ensuring financial support was forthcoming on a more generous basis than hitherto. But probably the most significant of the reforms was the introduction of a new design of lifeboat – the self-righter, based on Beeching's prize-winning design of 1851. All of the places in Cornwall that received new lifeboats in the 1850s and 1860s received this design of lifeboat. In fact, all of Cornwall's lifeboat stations operated a boat of this type at one time or another.

ABOVE: *Launching the Port Isaac lifeboat RICHARD AND SARAH (ON.334) across the beach. With no horses available, she was pushed into the water by a large team of helpers.*

BELOW: *Recovery of RICHARD AND SARAH at Port Isaac involved working in the village's narrow confined streets.*

The second half of the nineteenth century was the heyday of the self-righting lifeboat. The design had been perfected since its conception in 1851 so that, by the 1880s, it was almost the only type of lifeboat in use. Self-righters were primarily rowing boats, usually 34ft or 35ft in length, with a rather limited radius of action. For this reason, two lifeboats and sometimes more were operated at many stations. At the Lizard, although the flank stations established were relatively close to the initial station, in the 1880s it was deemed necessary to place a second boat at the station. This was operated from Church Cove, a small cove between Polpeor and Cadgwith, where a new lifeboat house was built. Two lifeboats were also operated at Padstow for more than 60 years. In 1901, a large lifeboat was sent to the station which was intended for long-range work attending casualties out to sea. The other boat was smaller and lighter, intended for work closer inshore and in the Camel estuary itself.

Launch of the Newquay lifeboat JAMES STEVENS No.5 (ON.426) down the steep slipway at Towan Head. The slipway was one of the steepest in the country and so the lifeboat had to be recovered on the beach and brought back to the boathouse by carriage. FROM AN OLD POSTCARD IN THE AUTHOR'S COLLECTION

During the nineteenth century, lifeboats were kept on the shore almost without exception, and therefore some method of quickly and easily getting them afloat when needed was vitally important. Usually, they would be launched from a carriage, down a slipway or over a beach on skids. Ensuring that a lifeboat successfully got afloat was clearly of crucial importance to the success of a rescue mission. The relatively light self-righting lifeboats were well suited to being launched from a carriage or over skids off an open beach. However, the effort needed to perform such an operation, in the days before mechanical launching aids, to get the boat afloat, often in the worst of weathers, was considerable. Lifeboats were at least 34ft in length, weighed two tons and often more, and so considerable numbers of shore helpers were needed particularly on gently shelving beaches such as those at St Ives and Penzance.

Because they were light enough to be carriage launched, and because sailing against the wind in a vessel relying solely on manpower was slow and exhausting work, these lifeboats would sometimes be taken further afield to a site from where a launch would enable the casualty to be reached more easily. At Padstow, an unusual and unique development involved a carriage being kept in a small house specially built in 1883 on high ground above the town for moving the lifeboat to one of the beaches around Padstow other than those usually used, often some distance away from the station.

Between 1865 and 1885, a further ten stations were established. On the south coast, new stations were opened at Looe (1866); Falmouth, Cadgwith and Mullion (all 1867); Mevagissey and Porthoustock (both 1869); Portloe (1870); and a No.2 station at Lizard (1885). On the north coast lifeboats were placed at Hayle (1866) and Port Isaac (1869). A second station was opened in the Isles of Scilly, at St Agnes, in 1890. This station was intended to assist vessels wrecked on the Western Rocks, the most dangerous part of the Isles of Scilly, but the local community was so small it was often difficult to obtain a full crew.

St Agnes lifeboat CHARLES DEERE JAMES (ON.590) on the special launching trolley which ran on rails down the slipways built at Priglis Bay in 1903. This lifeboat, of the 38ft Watson sailing design, served St Agnes from 1909 to 1920 when the station was closed

Porthoustock lifeboat men, wearing their cork life-jackets, outside the boathouse in front of the 33ft self-righter MARY ANN STORY, the first lifeboat to serve at the station. RNLI

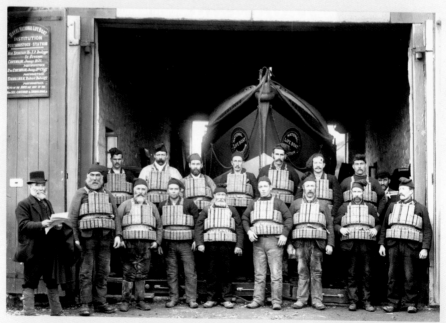

Because conditions in which lifeboats are often called to operate, nineteenth century lifeboat designers believed that a steam-powered lifeboat, then the only means of mechanical propulsion available, was impractical. Despite the advantages of steam power, designing and building a steam lifeboat presented designers with a completely different set of problems to those of pulling lifeboat design. However, advances in engineering techniques during the 1880s meant that building a steam powered lifeboat became a possibility.

By 1890, it became a reality when the first steam lifeboat, the *Duke of Northumberland*, was launched from her builder's yard on the Thames and made her first trial trip. During the next decade, the RNLI had a further five steam lifeboats built for service around the British Isles. These impressive vessels were all over 50ft in length and could cover a much greater area than any pulling or sailing lifeboat. However, their size severely restricted the number of places where they could be stationed as they had to be kept moored afloat, and unlike today there were fewer places where sheltered moorings could be taken up.

In Cornwall, Padstow was deemed the only suitable place from where such a vessel could operate and one was sent there in February 1899. She was 56ft 6in in length and was named *James Stevens No.4*. She was only the second lifeboat to be built that was driven by a single propeller – her sister ship, *James Stevens No.3*, was the first. Sadly, this vessel only served until April 1900, making just two services before she was tragically wrecked beyond repair.

The disaster that befell *James Stevens No.4* was one of the worst in the RNLI's history, for not only did the steam lifeboat capsize but the station's pulling lifeboat *Arab*, a 34ft self-righter, was also wrecked going to the same vessel. Both lifeboats put out on 11 April

The unique steam tug Helen Peele (ON.478), built for service at Padstow, worked in conjunction with the lifeboat Edmund Harvey. From an old postcard in the author's collection

Steam Lifeboat "Helen Peele", Padstow.

1900 to the ketch *Peace and Plenty*, of Lowestoft, which had anchored at the harbour mouth after having fished during the day. By nightfall, she began to drag her anchors, and eventually hit the shore. The Trebetherick Life Brigade fired a rocket line to the casualty and managed to drag four men ashore. Another jumped overboard and made it to the shore safely, but three others were drowned.

Meanwhile, *Arab* had launched to assist the ketch and searched for an hour. Unable to see anything in the prevailing conditions, the lifeboat crew set course to return to Padstow. But as they began the return journey, a very heavy sea struck the boat unseating the crew and breaking or carrying away nine of the ten oars. The crew threw the anchor overboard in the hope that it would hold the boat, while a distress flare was burnt to signal to the steam lifeboat that they were in trouble. They then succeeded in beaching the boat using the spare oars and all managed to safely scramble ashore.

During this time, *James Stevens No.4* was putting out with the intention of helping the ketch. As her draught was too great for a direct crossing of the sands in the estuary, a course was set out for deeper water. However, before managing to turn towards the casualty, she was caught by a huge sea which lifted her stern completely out of the water. She was spun broadside to the waves and turned over. The seven crewmen in the cockpit were thrown clear but the four in the engine room tending the boilers were trapped. Three of the men washed off the boat were washed ashore and subsequently revived but the other four were lost. The lifeboat itself was thrown into a small cave in the rocks at Hell Bay. She resembled, one onlooker commented the following day, 'nothing so much as a battered tin can'.

Despite the loss of *James Stevens No.4*, a powered lifeboat was still deemed necessary for the conditions in Padstow harbour. So, the RNLI had a steam tug built to work alongside a large pulling lifeboat in what was a unique combination. Commercially operated steam tugs were used in life-saving at other major ports, notably Ramsgate, where the lifeboat would be towed to the scene of a wreck and thus reduce the effort needed by the crew. However as no such tug was available at Padstow, the RNLI built one to their own specification. Named *Helen Peele*, she was 95ft 6in long, built of steel, and had two compound engines producing 400hp, which drove twin screws. During her trials she developed a speed of over 10 knots, which was seen as very satisfactory.

FREDERICK H. PILLEY (ON.657) about to be recovered at Polpero Cove, Lizard. A 38ft motor self-righter, she was one of the first motor lifeboats to operate in Cornwall, and was stationed at Lizard from 1920 to 1938 during which time she saved 130 lives. FROM AN OLD POSTCARD IN THE AUTHOR'S COLLECTION

The scene at Padstow during a lifeboat day in the early years of the twentieth century with the 36ft self-righter ARAB (ON.472), on the left, by Customs House slipway and the larger 42ft self-righter EDMUND HARVEY. (ON.475) The station at Padstow has a complicated history and operated at least two lifeboats for a number of years. FROM AN OLD POSTCARD IN THE AUTHOR'S COLLECTION

Helen Peele was one of three new boats the RNLI provided for Padstow following the tragedy of 1900. The other two were both standard self-righting pulling lifeboats of differing sizes. The larger one, a 42ft twelve-oared boat named *Edmund Harvey*, was used in conjunction with *Helen Peele* and, with the steam tug, was kept at moorings off Hawker's Cove. These two boats undertook much life-saving work and operated together successfully throughout the twenty-eight years they were stationed at Padstow. The smaller boat, 36ft by 8ft 3in and ten-oared, was named *Arab* and was kept on a carriage in the house at Hawker's Cove from where she was launched. She was intended to cover the estuary and work more closely to the shore than the larger moored lifeboats.

INTO THE TWENTIETH CENTURY

The introduction of motor power to lifeboats during the early years of the twentieth century was a significant advance. Although, lifeboatmen using the pulling and sailing lifeboats often performed remarkable and extraordinary feats of life-saving, a powered lifeboat would provide distinct benefits and offer definite advantages over a lifeboat relying on sails, oars or a combination of the two. As steam was poorly suited to power lifeboats, the newly invented internal combustion engine offered greater potential.

Petrol-driven engines were developed during the second half of the nineteenth century, and used to power motor vehicles in the 1880s. By the 1900s, it was inevitable that motor power, in the form of the internal combustion engine, would become

THE THREE SISTERS (ON.771), a 35ft 6in single-engined Liverpool motor lifeboat that served Coverack from 1934 to 1954.

1904 A lifeboat is converted to motor for the first time.

1909 The first purpose-built motor lifeboat completed.

1918 First motor lifeboat in Cornwall enters service.

1932 First lifeboat fitted with a diesel engine which offers greater range and better fuel economy.

1967 The 44ft Waveney, based on a United States Coast Guard design, introduced into service to become the RNLI's first design of fast lifeboat.

1979 First 52ft Arun sent to Cornwall and stationed at Falmouth. The Arun was introduced by the RNLI in the 1970s and became one of the most successful lifeboat designs ever.

1994 New 25-knot designs of lifeboat, the 17m Severn and 14m Trent, entered service.

Launch of the Cadgwith motor lifeboat GUIDE OF DUNKIRK (ON.826) across skids laid on the beach. She was the only motor lifeboat to serve the station which was closed in 1963 after a new lifeboat station had been built at Kilcobben Cove for a larger and more powerful lifeboat. RNLI

a vital element in life-saving. In 1904, a lifeboat was fitted with an engine for the first time. Although there were many problems to be overcome to successfully operate an engine on board a lifeboat, once numerous setbacks and technical problems had been solved, lifeboats powered by the internal combustion engine pointed the way ahead.

Initially lifeboats already in service were converted with the fitting of an engine but in 1908 the first lifeboat built with an engine was completed and entered service the following year in Orkney. Further developments with engines were delayed by the

The 45ft 6in Watson motor W. & S. (ON.736) being launched down the slipway from the boathouse at Penlee Point. She served at Penlee from 1931 to 1960 and saved 87 lives during that time.

Lizard lifeboat DUKE OF YORK (ON.769), a 41ft Watson motor type, returns to the lifeboat house at Polpeor Cove. RNLI

war of 1914-18, but once hostilities had ended the RNLI made up for lost time with an ambitious building programme. The first motor lifeboat in Cornwall was stationed at the Lizard in 1918, and another went to St Mary's the following year. Sennen Cove and Penlee both received new motor lifeboats in 1922, and during the years between the two world wars, motor lifeboats were sent to ten of Cornwall's lifeboat stations.

Motor lifeboats were stationed at places where they could be manned and launched most efficiently. As they could cover a greater area than their pulling counterparts, many of the stations established during the nineteenth century, and which operated the standard self-righter, were closed when a neighbouring station received a motor lifeboat. Although this led to a reduction in the number of stations in the county, the actual area covered by the new motor lifeboats was greater and the danger spots could be reached more quickly than ever.

Falmouth received a motor lifeboat in 1931, a year after the station at Mevagissey was closed. The station at Polkerris was transferred to nearby Fowey, the preferred location for a lifeboat to cover St Austell Bay. A motor lifeboat could leave the estuary at Fowey in all weathers, something a pulling lifeboat could not achieve. After St Mary's received a motor lifeboat in 1919, the other station on the Isles of Scilly, St Agnes, was closed. And with two motor lifeboats operating from Padstow by the early 1930s, Port Isaac lifeboat was withdrawn in 1933. By the end of the

Launch of 42ft Watson motor WILLIAM TAYLOR OF OLDHAM (ON.907) on 24 July 1954, the day she arrived at Coverack. The station's previous lifeboat, THE THREE SISTERS, is moored on the right. The station was closed in 1979.

21

The impressive twin-screwed 61ft Barnett PRINCESS MARY (ON.715) at moorings off Hawker's Cove, Padstow. The schooner on her beam ends in the background is MARIA REGINA, which ran aground in March 1932. GRAHAM FARR COLLECTION

Second World War, there were ten lifeboat stations in Cornwall, all operating motor lifeboats: Fowey, Falmouth, Coverack, Cadgwith, Lizard, Penlee, Sennen Cove, St Mary's, St Ives and Padstow.

Most immediate post-war lifeboats were based on old designs of pulling and sailing lifeboats, but were fitted with a single engine driving a single propeller. The Lizard's new motor lifeboat, *Sir Fitzroy Clayton*, the first such boat in Cornwall and one of the first motor lifeboats ever built, was based on the self-righting pulling lifeboat. She was 38ft in length and fitted with a single 35hp Tylor petrol engine. Built in 1912, she had been stationed at Newhaven until coming to the Lizard in 1918. In this boat, the crew gained valuable experience while their own motor lifeboat, *Frederick H. Pilley*, was under construction at Cowes. This new boat, also a 38ft self-righter, arrived at the Lizard in November 1920. She was fitted with a single 45hp Tylor JB4 petrol engine, which gave her a top speed of more than seven knots.

At Sennen Cove, the new motor lifeboat was also a self-righter, 40ft in length, but at both St Mary's and Penlee the newly designed 45ft Watson class of lifeboat, a larger and more powerful type, went on station. The Watson motor lifeboats were similar to their pulling counterparts in that they had greater overall stability, although they were not self-righting. As the RNLI gained greater experience in the operation of motor lifeboats, and more reliable and powerful engines were developed, larger boats were designed, such as the 45ft Watson class, which were able to cover a greater area than ever before.

An even larger type was introduced in the 1920s when James Barnett, the RNLI's Consulting Naval Engineer, designed a 60ft lifeboat that employed twin engines and twin propellers, eliminating the need for the auxiliary sails that single engined motor lifeboats carried. The lifeboat types that he designed were large twin engined non-self-righting boats, and these became the mainstay of the lifeboat fleet for many decades. Only four of the large 60ft Barnett motor lifeboats were built, one of which, *Princess Mary*, was stationed at Padstow in May 1929 and did excellent service there until 1952.

Although most of Cornwall's lifeboat stations were established during the latter half of the nineteenth century, there have been new stations founded during the twentieth century, and some well established stations relocated. A new station was founded in 1901 at Coverack following shipwrecks on the Manacles in 1898 and 1899. A house and slipway were built which enabled the lifeboat to be launched quickly and easily, and the station received a motor lifeboat in 1934. At this time, slipway launching was seen as the best way of getting a lifeboat afloat, whereas sheltered deep-water moorings are

Arrival at Sennen Cove of the station's first motor lifeboat, the 40ft motor self-righter THE NEWBONS (ON.674), pictured approaching the double slipway arrangement and boathouse. She served at Sennen from 1922 to 1948. RNLI

46ft 9in Watson motor Deneys Reitz (ON.919), with her cockpit enclosed and radar fitted, at sea off Fowey. She was on station there from 1954 to 1980. Paul Richards

regarded as the ideal today. However, where a sheltered mooring is not available, slipways are a viable alternative.

A number of new lifeboat houses with slipways have been built at existing stations in Cornwall during the twentieth century to overcome the difficulty of launching a lifeboat in heavy weather and strong winds. The first new house was constructed at Penlee Point in 1913. With a steep slipway, this house enabled a fast launch for a lifeboat that was larger and heavier than any that could be accommodated on a carriage, the launch method hitherto favoured at Penzance. This boathouse served Penlee station for seventy years and is still maintained, located on the road between Newlyn and Mousehole.

Perhaps the most significant changes to already established stations took place at Padstow and The Lizard, where new lifeboat houses and roller slipways were built at specially selected sites. In the late 1950s at it was decided to amalgamate the Lizard and Cadgwith stations. A site was selected at Kilcobben Cove, a mile and a quarter to the east of the Lizard lighthouse, which was sufficiently sheltered to enable a new lifeboat house and slipway to be built. Careful visual and instrumental observations were carried out at the site between winter 1957 and spring 1958. These showed that it would be possible to launch a lifeboat at this point in any weather and at any state of the tide, and that conditions for re-housing would usually be favourable. The foundation stone was laid on 23 November 1959, and the new house was formally opened on 13 July 1961 by the Duke of Edinburgh. The new station had cost £100,000 and consisted of a boathouse and slipway near foot of cliffs approached down the cliffs by about 200 steps.

A similar investment was made by the RNLI at Padstow during the 1960s following serious problems with the silting up of the Doom Bar which made launching extremely difficult from the boathouse at Hawker's Cove and the nearby moorings. Wave recordings taken over a period of two years at Trevose Head showed that a slipway station built at this location would enable a launch in any weather conditions. In 1965 the decision to build the new station there was made. It was completed in two years at a cost of approximately £114,600 and became operational on 23 October 1967. It was similar to the station at the Lizard, and consisted of a boathouse and slipway on the foreshore at the foot of the cliffs with a slipway 240ft in length.

While new stations have been built in Cornwall, there has also been continued modernisation of the lifeboat fleet since 1945. This is reflected not only in the introduction of the inshore lifeboat, described below, but also by the considerable advances in the design of all

The lifeboat house and slipway built at Kilcobben Cove in 1959-61 for the Lizard lifeboat, with 47ft Tyne David Robinson (ON.1145) on the slipway. The inclined railway up the cliff was installed for ease of access. Nicholas Leach

weather lifeboats. Probably the most significant advance has seen the introduction of the 'fast' lifeboats capable of a speed much greater than the eight or nine knots managed by the first generation of motor lifeboats. In 1963, the RNLI purchased a 44ft steel hulled lifeboat from the United States Coast Guard service and following successful trials a building programme was embarked upon. This boat, self-righting by virtue of its watertight wheelhouse, was faster than the conventional lifeboats then in service and completely different from the traditional British lifeboat designs. The type was given the class name Waveney, and it was the first of the modern generation of 'fast' lifeboats.

12m Mersey The Four Boys (ON.1176) launching from Sennen Cove in April 1992 at the end of her dedication ceremony. Funded by the Land's End Lifeboat Appeal, she was named in memory of the four Stoke Poges schoolboys lost off Land's End in 1985. Tim Stevens

In the late 1960s the RNLI believed that a slightly larger and faster lifeboat was needed, so new 50ft and 52ft types were developed. The 52ft design became the Arun class, and the 50ft design was named the Thames class. The first 'fast' lifeboat to go on station in Cornwall was the prototype Thames class boat *Rotary Service*, which was stationed at Falmouth in 1974. However, the Arun proved to be a better boat and since its inception has become one of the finest lifeboat types ever developed for use by the RNLI. Capable of a speed between 18 and 20 knots, the Arun represented a radical departure for lifeboat design and was completely different from anything that had gone before. In 1978, a new 52ft Arun, named *Elizabeth Ann*, was sent to Falmouth where she served with great distinction. Another Arun was stationed at St Mary's in 1981 where the slipway launch was abandoned in favour of a mooring in the harbour. A further Arun was

Padstow lifeboat James Burrough (ON.1094) on exercise with a Sea King SAR helicopter in the Camel Estuary. Nicholas Leach

With St Michael's Mount behind, relief 52ft Arun *A. J. R. AND L. G. URIDGE (ON.1086)* leads the new 17m Severn *IVAN ELLEN (ON.1265)* into Newlyn harbour on 11 March 2003 as the new boat arrives at her station. NICHOLAS LEACH

stationed at Penlee in 1983, moored in the fishing harbour at Newlyn.

The introduction of the Waveney and Arun 'fast' lifeboats in the 1960s and 70s marked the beginning of the modernisation undertaken by the RNLI. However, at stations where boats could not be moored afloat other designs of 'fast' lifeboat were needed. So, in the 1980s, two new classes were introduced: the 47ft Tyne and 12m Mersey, intended for stations which practised slipway and carriage launching respectively. In Cornwall, one of the first of the Tynes went on station at Padstow in 1984, and in 1988 another was stationed at The Lizard. The 12m Mersey class was introduced in the late 1980s, and in 1990 one was stationed at St Ives, where an impressive new lifeboat house was built to accommodate the new boat, inshore lifeboat and crew facilities.

As lifeboats are kept at moorings at the majority of stations in Britain and Ireland, during the early 1990s an even faster breed of lifeboat intended to be kept afloat was introduced. The new designs, the 14m Trent and 17m Severn, are capable of reaching speeds up to 25 knots which means that the time taken to reach a casualty will be reduced by nearly 30 per cent. The first boats of these new types were ordered in 1992 and began entering service in the mid-1990s. Cornwall has only three all weather stations where it is possible to moor the lifeboat afloat, and these soon received the new designs. A Trent, named *Maurice and Joyce Hardy*, went on station at Fowey in October 1996; Severns were placed at Falmouth in January 1997 and St Mary's in December 1997. Trents and Severns will ensure that the RNLI can continue to provide a comprehensive sea rescue service into the twenty-first century. In 2005, they were joined by the Tamar class, another 25-knot design, intended to operate from slipway stations. One of the first of the new Tamars was allocated to Padstow where, alongside the existing house, a new lifeboat house was constructed in 2005-6 big enough to take the new design.

17m Severn THE WHITEHEADS (ON.1229) on exercise off the Isles of Scilly. Built in 1997, she was the first of the new generation of 25-knot fast lifeboats to be stationed in Cornwall, operating from the key station at St Mary's. NICHOLAS LEACH

LIFEBOATS ON STATION: SOUTH

Looe. Atlantic 75 B-793 *Alan and Margaret,* on station 2.10.2003, carriage.
D class inflatable D-574 *Regina Mary,* on station 5.3.2002, trolley.

Fowey. 14m Trent ON.1222 (14-18) *Maurice and Joyce Hardy,* on station 10.10.1996, afloat.
D class inflatable D-526, *Olive Herbert,* on station 30.9.1997, trolley and davit.

Falmouth. 17m Severn ON.1256 (17-29) *Richard Cox Scott,* on station 18.12.2001, afloat.
Atlantic 21 B-595 *Falmouth Round Table,* on station 9.3.1994, trolley.

The Lizard. 47ft Tyne ON.1145 (47-030) *David Robinson,* on station 17.8.1988, slipway.

Penlee. 17m Severn ON.1265 (17-36) *Ivan Ellen,* on station 15.3.2003, afloat.
Atlantic 75 B-787 *Paul Alexander,* on station 16.8.2002, carriage.

St Mary's (Isles of Scilly). 17m Severn ON.1229 (17-11) *The Whiteheads,* on station 1.12.1997, afloat.

Sennen Cove. 47ft Tyne ON.1121 (47-016) *Norman Salvesen,* on station 5.12.1998, slipway.
D class inflatable D-624 *Spirit of the RLC,* on station 22.7.2004, trolley.

Norman Salvesen at Sennen Cove. Nicholas Leach

N

0   5 miles
0   5 km

ST MARTIN'S
BRYHER
TRESCO
HUGH TOWN
ST AGNES
ST MARY'S

ISLES OF SCILLY
28 miles / 45 km off Land's End

● **LOCATION OF LIFEBOAT STATIONS**

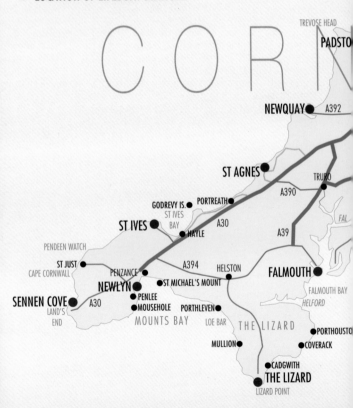

CORN

TREVOSE HEAD
PADSTO

NEWQUAY   A392

ST AGNES
TRURO
A390
FAL
GODREVY IS.
PORTREATH
ST IVES BAY
A30
A39
ST IVES
HAYLE
PENDEEN WATCH
ST JUST
CAPE CORNWALL
A394
HELSTON
FALMOUTH
PENZANCE
FALMOUTH BAY
HELFORD
NEWLYN
ST MICHAEL'S MOUNT
SENNEN COVE
A30
PENLEE
PORTHLEVEN
PORTHOUSTO
LAND'S END
MOUSEHOLE
COVERACK
MOUNTS BAY
LOE BAR
THE LIZARD
MULLION
CADGWITH
THE LIZARD
LIZARD POINT

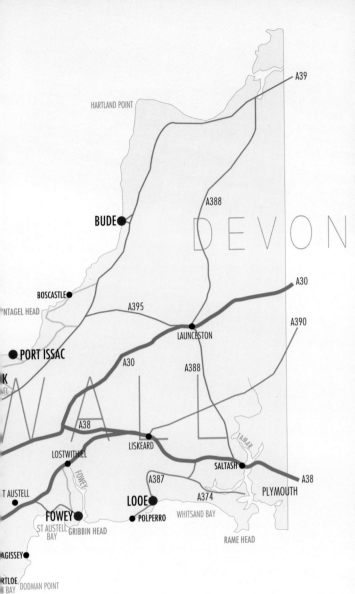

HARTLAND POINT

A39

A388

D E V O N

BUDE

BOSCASTLE

NTAGEL HEAD

A395

A30

LAUNCESTON

A390

PORT ISSAC

A30

A388

K

W A L L

A38

LOSTWITHIEL

LISKEARD

SALTASH

TAMAR

A38

T AUSTELL

FOWEY

A387

LOOE

A374

POLPERRO

WHITSAND BAY

PLYMOUTH

ST AUSTELL
BAY

GRIBBIN HEAD

RAME HEAD

AGISSEY

RTLOE
BAY

DODMAN POINT

*St Ives 12m Mersey
lifeboat* THE PRINCESS ROYAL
at sea. PAUL RICHARDS

LIFEBOATS ON STATION: NORTH

St Ives. 12m Mersey ON.1167 (12-009) *The Princess Royal (Civil Service No.41)*, on station 23.10.1990, carriage.
D class inflatable D-515, *Spirit of the RCT*, on station 8.5.1997, trolley and quadbike.

St Agnes. D class inflatable D-641, *Blue Peter IV*, on station 1.3.2005, trolley and quadbike.

Newquay. Atlantic 75 B-715 *Phyllis*, on station 14.8.1995, carriage.
D class inflatable D-636 *Valerie Wilson*, on station 17.2.2005, trolley and quadbike.

Padstow. 47ft Tyne ON.1094 (47-003) *James Burrough*, on station 28.12.1984, slipway.

Rock. D class inflatable D-634 *Rusper*, on station 1.2.2005, trolley and quadbike.

Port Isaac. D class inflatable D-546 *Spirit of the PCS RE II*, on station 3.6.1999, trolley and quadbike.

Bude. D class inflatable D-617 *Henry Philip*, on station 11.5.2005, trolley and tractor.

Details correct as at 31.12.2005

Throughout the history of the RNLI, the pattern of lifeboat coverage has changed in response to changing demands on the service. Before the 1960s, when few people could afford yachts or motor boats and wind-sailing and surfing were almost unknown, lifeboats were most needed by commercial and fishing vessels. But during the 1960s, as more people began using the sea for leisure, the number of inshore incidents to which lifeboats were called increased. Conventional lifeboats were not well suited to dealing with such incidents and a fast rescue craft was required that could respond speedily to incidents when a few minutes could make the difference between life and death.

D class inflatable D-453 BLUE PETER IV returns to St Agnes after exercise. The station is one of seven whose lifeboat is funded by the BBC Television programme. NICHOLAS LEACH

To meet the demand for a small fast type of lifeboat, the RNLI bought an inflatable boat in 1962 for extensive trials, and a delegation visited France, where similar boats were in operation, to obtain further advice and see the boats in service. Following these initial steps, the first inshore rescue boats (IRBs) were introduced during the summer of 1963. Such was the success of these boats during that summer more and more places began to operate the boats in subsequent years. The first IRB to go on station in Cornwall was placed at St Ives in 1964.

The 16ft inflatable lifeboats, made from tough nylon with neoprene, were crewed by two, powered by a 40hp outboard engine, and could be launched quickly and easily. The advantages of these boats were their speed, which at 20 knots was considerably faster than any lifeboat in service during the 1960s, the ability to go alongside other craft or persons in the water without causing or suffering damage and the short time taken to launch.

Some stations that had been established during the nineteenth century, but closed following the advent of the motor lifeboat, were reopened to operate an inshore lifeboat (ILB, as they became known). At Newquay, where the motor lifeboat had been withdrawn in 1945, an ILB became operational in 1965. It was found to be ideally suited to working

C class inflatable C-512 returns to Newquay after a service launch in August 1992. Newquay and St Ives both operated twin-engined C class inflatables during the 1980s and 1990s. NICHOLAS LEACH

in the heavy surf encountered off the beaches of the north Cornwall coast. Further ILB stations were established on the north coast at Bude in 1966 and Port Isaac in 1967, stations that had previously operated pulling lifeboats..

The first station to solely operate an ILB was at St Agnes, also on the north coast, which became operational in April 1968. The station's ILB is one of those funded by the various Blue Peter appeals. The first of these appeals was launched on 5 December 1966, and it was so successful that four inshore lifeboats were provided, one of which – *Blue Peter IV* – went to St Agnes. There have been a number of Blue Peter appeals since then, most recent in 1993/4, called 'Pieces of Eight', which again proved a huge success. The latest Blue Peter funded lifeboat at St Agnes went on station in February 1994.

While the inflatable ILB proved to be very successful, by the late 1960s there was a requirement for a larger inshore lifeboat, capable of night operation with a greater range. After various rigid hulls had been tested, one developed at Atlantic College in South Wales was deemed the most suitable. The boat had a rigid wooden hull with an inflatable sponson attached to it, and had twin outboard engines fitted which enabled a speed of over 30 knots to be achieved, while the sponsons gave the boat great

The crew of Bude's IB1 inshore lifeboat D-617 HENRY PHILIP negotiate surf off Summerleaze beach. NICHOLAS LEACH

stability. The new design was refined by the RNLI, and in 1972 the first of the class, known as the Atlantic 21, went on station. Atlantics have since been stationed at Falmouth and Newquay, where they have proved ideal craft for the casualties dealt with at each station.

During the 1990s, the number of inshore lifeboat stations in Cornwall increased to improve the coverage of parts of the coastline where increased number of rescues suitable for an ILB have occurred. The Marazion station, located at St Michael's Mount, was opened in 1990 as an extension of the Penzance and Penlee station. In 1994, a new station was opened at Rock, to cover the dangerous Camel estuary. The success of the one year evaluation led to the station becoming established on a permanent basis. Furthermore, ILBs have been stationed at Sennen Cove (in 1994) and Fowey (in 1995) to complement the all weather lifeboats already on station there. At Newquay, when the station was upgraded 1995 to operate an Atlantic 75, a D class inflatable was also supplied so the station now operates two inshore lifeboats.

Inshore lifeboats have proved to be a great success. Every year they carry out a great many rescues and save many people in difficulty. The following rescue, performed by one Newquay's two ILBs, shows why this type of craft has become such a vital element in the lifeboat service. On 26 March 1997, cries for help were heard coming from the bottom of the cliffs at Fern Cove and the station's D class ILB was launched just after 4pm. A man, who had been injured after falling down the cliff face, a woman and a 14-year-old boy were trapped by incoming tides, unable to climb to safety over slippery rocks. After

The scene at Looe on 18 October 2003 during the naming of Atlantic 75 B-793 ALAN AND MARGARET and opening of the new ILB house. Fowey and Plymouth all-weather lifeboats were in attendance, together with the restored pulling lifeboat RYDER, once stationed at Looe. PAUL RICHARDS

spotting the casualty, the ILB was beached on shingle amongst the rocks, while a Coastguard team was lowered from the cliff top. It was too risky to lift the family up the cliff, so they were lowered to the ILB in the surf below, while an RAF helicopter also provided help. Two of the three casualties were lifted off by helicopter, but the injured man was lowered to the ILB. The ILB crew struggled to hold their boat on the rocks in the heavy surf, but eventually managed to get the casualty on board. To get out of the small cover, they had to fight through 250 yards of breaking surf. Once clear, the casualties were transferred to Newquay's Atlantic 75 that was standing by and then rushed to hospital. The RNLI's Thanks on Vellum was accorded to the ILB's three crew members who worked as a team throughout the difficult rescue.

BEACH RESCUE

In 2000, the RNLI added another element to its life-saving services with the introduction of the Beach Lifeguard service. In September 2000, a pilot scheme was undertaken to evaluate the potential for expansion into beach lifeguarding around the UK. A pilot Beach Rescue service, later designated Beach Lifeguards, covered 26 beaches in the central south and south west of England with the aim of providing a 'joined-up service'. Between 2001 and 2004, the service was introduced to an increasing number of beaches so that it covered eight local authorities on 57 beaches in Hampshire, Devon and Cornwall. The new service was particularly

Arancia rescue boat A-28 and surfboard employed by the Beach Rescue team at Harlyn Bay. NICHOLAS LEACH

well represented in Cornwall with the Caradon, Carrick, Restormel and North Cornwall districts coming under the RNLI Beach Lifeguards service umbrella.

The number of lifeguards, and type and amount of equipment, varies depending on the local need, and is determined by a risk assessment of the beach. At selected beaches on the Cornish coast, the RNLI manages and organises the lifeguarding service. Each Beach Lifeguard Unit is equipped with radios, rescue boards, rescue tubes, oxygen, spinal boards and collars, a defibrillator and various other items of essential lifesaving equipment. Depending on the need, many beaches operate a four-wheel drive vehicle, an all-terrain vehicle, an Arancia inshore rescue boat, and a rescue water craft.

The Arancia rescue boat A-24 at Mawgam Porth ready despite the overcast weather. NICHOLAS LEACH

The Beach Rescue post at Porthcothan with four-wheel drive vehicle. NICHOLAS LEACH

The crews that man the lifeboats are and always have been volunteers and this aspect of the lifeboat service makes them special in the eyes of the public. They perform heroic and courageous acts in the course of their duty. Of the many rescues performed by the men and women who operate Cornwall's lifeboats, it is impossible to claim any one particular service is the most notable but many outstanding rescues have been completed.

Many rescues have already been described, but the following wartime incident exemplifies the courage and bravery exhibited by the lifeboat crews of Cornwall. On 19 January 1940, in a south-easterly gale and very heavy seas, the steamship *Kirkpool*, of West Hartlepool, started dragging her anchors off Castle Reach in Falmouth Bay. The Falmouth lifeboat *Crawford and Constance Conybeare* went to her aid as she had struck the beach and lay broadside on with seas breaking against her. Tugs were unable to get close enough so the lifeboat went in to take off those on board.

Despite heavy seas, Coxswain John Snell drove the lifeboat through the surf round the bows of the steamer to get between casualty and shore. Once in position, Snell placed the lifeboat alongside the steamer, took off an injured man as well as thirteen other men and landed them at Falmouth. He then went back to the steamer and, with seas breaking right over her, repeated the manoeuvre to rescue the other twenty-one on board. The Silver medal was awarded to Coxswain Snell for his skill in handling the lifeboat, and the Bronze medal went to the mechanic, Charles Williams.

In addition to the many acts of bravery, several tragedies have occurred to the lifeboats of Cornwall which have resulted in lifeboatmen losing their lives. The disaster which overtook Padstow's two lifeboats in April 1900 has already been described, but a number of other lifeboatmen have given their lives in the course of duty. The tragedies that overtook the St Ives station in the late 1930s are unparalleled in the history of the RNLI: within the space of twelve months two lifeboats and twelve lives had been tragically lost.

The first accident occurred on 31 January 1938 when the small motor lifeboat *Caroline Parsons*, manned by a crew of nine, went to the aid of the steamer *Alba*. In very heavy seas, twenty-three men were taken off the casualty but, as the lifeboat was leaving the scene, she was hit broadside on by a huge wave and capsized. The lifeboat righted herself but was driven onto the rocks. The lifeboatmen on board managed to get ashore with

St Ives lifeboat JOHN AND SARAH ELIZA STYCH *(ON.743) ashore near Godrevy on 23 January 1939 after capsizing on service with the loss of seven lives.* FROM AN OLD PHOTO IN THE AUTHOR'S COLLECTION

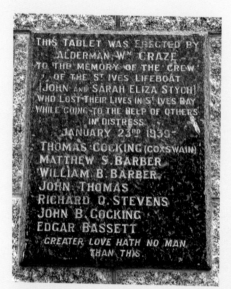

Plaque mounted on the lifeboat house at St Ives in memory of those lost in the 1939 disaster. NICHOLAS LEACH

the aid of the life-saving apparatus but the rescued men were not so fortunate and five died. Following this fatal mishap, another lifeboat, *John and Sarah Eliza Stych*, formerly at the Padstow No.2 station, was sent to St Ives. Sadly, she was to serve for less than a year before being lost in another disaster.

In the early hours of 23 January 1939, *John and Sarah Eliza Stych* was launched to the aid of an unknown vessel in difficulty two miles off Cape Cornwall. Encountering very heavy seas once out of the shelter of St Ives Head, she was capsized and four of the eight men on board were lost, including the Coxswain Thomas Cocking. Although the boat righted herself, the engine could not be restarted and so she drifted helplessly before the storm with no power. Fruitless attempts were made to restart the engine, but when another big sea hit her she again capsized. This time, the motor mechanic was lost leaving only three survivors on board the disabled lifeboat which drifted towards Godrevy out of control. As she approached the rocks, another sea hit her and for a third time she was capsized. After righting again, only one man, William Freeman, remained on her. He had only survived by forcing himself under the canopy above the engine controls. When the lifeboat was thrown ashore by the sea at Godrevy, Freeman crawled out and reached a local farm, from where news of the disaster was sent to St Ives. This second disaster was worse than the first – seven out of the eight lifeboatmen on board were drowned. It hit the small community of St Ives hard, and the lifeboat station was temporarily closed.

Another tragedy in Cornwall occurred in December 1981 when the Penlee lifeboat *Solomon Browne* was wrecked on service to the coaster *Union Star*. The lifeboat had launched to the coaster in hurricane force winds and mountainous seas, and succeeded in approaching the vessel to take off four of the eight people on board. However, in going back to the vessel to rescue the remaining people, the lifeboat was overwhelmed and all on board were lost. Nobody saw exactly what happened, and despite an extensive search throughout the following days nobody was found alive.

At the subsequent Inquest, the following letter, sent to the RNLI from Lieut Commander Russell Smith USN, pilot of the helicopter involved in the rescue attempts, was read. It provides the most moving account of the rescue attempted by the crew of *Solomon Browne*: 'Throughout the entire rescue evolution the Penlee crew never appeared to hesitate. After each time they were washed, blown of bumped away from the casualty the Penlee immediately commenced another run in. Their spirit and dedication was amazing. The greatest act of courage that I have ever seen, and am ever

Memorial in Padstow cemetery to the lifeboatmen lost in the disaster of April 1900. NICHOLAS LEACH

Launch of the ill-fated Penlee lifeboat SOLOMON BROWNE (ON.954) down the slipway at Penlee Point from where she launched in December 1981 to the coaster UNION STAR. FROM AN PHOTO IN THE AUTHOR'S COLLECTION

likely to see, was the penultimate courage and dedication shown by the Penlee when it manoeuvred back alongside the casualty in over 60ft breakers and rescuing four people shortly after the Penlee had been bashed on top of the casualty's hatch covers. They were truly the bravest eight men I've ever seen who were also totally dedicated to upholding the highest standards of the RNLI.' The RNLI awarded the Gold medal posthumously to Coxswain William Trevelyan Richards, and Bronze medals to each of the seven crew lost on that dreadful night in December 1981.

Like the tragedy at St Ives in 1939, events at Penlee greatly affected the small village of Mousehole from where all eight members of the crew came. Yet in spite of the great loss suffered by this small community, men immediately volunteered to form a new crew and operate another lifeboat. At first a relief lifeboat was supplied until a new lifeboat had been built for the station and on 18 July 1983 the Arun class vessel *Mabel Alice* was named and dedicated at a moving ceremony. Such dedication and devotion to the task of saving life at sea demonstrated by those at Penlee is testimony to the courage and selflessness of lifeboat crews not only in Cornwall, but throughout the British Isles.

Gold Medal Service plaque displayed inside the present lifeboat crew room at Newlyn Harbour.
NICHOLAS LEACH

CORNWALL'S LIFEBOAT STATIONS

The gazetteer is arranged in geographical order from Looe, in south east Cornwall, along the coast west to Land's End and the Isles of Scilly, then up the north coast as far as Bude, the most northerly lifeboat station in Cornwall. Details of the station's current operational lifeboats have been included, and these are accurate as at 31 December 2005.

LOOE. A lifeboat station was established at Looe by the RNLI in 1866 and a lifeboat house was built on the beach at East Looe near the harbour entrance. The house, which had unusual ornamental features, was used until the station closed in 1930. It is still standing, little altered externally, having had a variety of uses.

In 1992 the station was reopened and operated a D class inflatable. This was housed in a building on the beach adjacent to the old boathouse until 1998 when a new ILB house was opened at Middleton's Corner, East Looe Quay. From this house, the ILB could be davit-launched into the river or taken through the streets to the beach.

Following trials with an Atlantic inshore lifeboat in 2001, the station was upgraded to operate both Atlantic and D class ILBs. To accommodate the new set-up, a new ILB house was built in 2002-3 for an Atlantic 75, its launching vehicle and the D class inflatable. The new house, sited on East Looe Quay on the site of a crazy golf course, incorporated crew room, shower and toilet facilities and was finished in local stone, granite and slate. The boat slipway into the river was also rebuilt.

With the completion of the new boathouse, relief Atlantic 75 B-700 was sent to the station for crew training. The station's own Atlantic 75, B-793 *Alan and Margaret*, was placed on station on 2 October 2003 and formally named and dedicated on 18 October 2003.

The lifeboat house at Looe built in 2002-3 at East Looe Quay for the Atlantic 75, D class inflatable and launching vehicles. NICHOLAS LEACH

In attendance at the ceremony was the station's former lifeboat *Ryder* (ON.489), which has been restored to her former glory, is on display at nearby Polperro. She was the last pulling lifeboat at Looe, and served from 1902 to 1930. She has been fully restored having been acquired by the Polperro Heritage Museum who saved her from destruction.

FOWEY. Fowey lifeboat station was established in 1922 and took over from Polkerris. In 1928 a motor lifeboat was placed on station, named *C. D. E. C.*, and kept moored afloat just off the town quay. No boathouse was built, but a building was found for the gear close to the town quay.

Looe lifeboats Atlantic 75 B-793 ALAN AND MARGARET and D class inflatable D-574 REGINA MARY on exercise. NICHOLAS LEACH

Fowey's D class inflatable D-526 OLIVER HERBERT at full speed. NICHOLAS LEACH

Fowey lifeboat 14m TRENT *MAURICE AND JOYCE* HARDY *(ON.1222) passing the Gribbin Head daymark marking the eastern end of St Austell Bay.* NICHOLAS LEACH

14m Trent MAURICE AND JOYCE HARDY *moored in the river with the ILB house and facility at Fowey, background right.* NICHOLAS LEACH

The service boards were displayed outside the Royal British Legion Club facing the Quay but have been moved.

In the 1990s, new moorings were found for the all-weather lifeboat upstream. In 1995, an ILB station was established on a summer only basis, and a D class inflatable was supplied. This was launched by davit from a site close to the lifeboat moorings. In 1997 a new purpose-built crew facility and ILB house was completed opposite the lifeboat moorings on the landward side of the road. The new Trent lifeboat, new ILB and new crew building were all dedicated at a unique triple ceremony on 4 October 1997.

POLKERRIS. Polkerris lifeboat station was established in 1859 by the RNLI to cover St Austell Bay. It was originally known as Fowey, despite being actually located at Polkerris. A lifeboat house, built for the first lifeboat, was used until 1903 when a new house was built on the beach. This second house remained in service until the station closed in 1922 and operations were transferred to nearby Fowey,

One of two service boards from the Polkerris station now mounted on display inside the old lifeboat house, which is used as a cafe. NICHOLAS LEACH

Launch of the Polkerris lifeboat James, WILLIAM AND CAROLINE COURTNEY *(ON.515) across the beach.* JOHN CORIN COLLECTION

The old lifeboat house at Polkerris built in 1903 and used until the station closed in 1922 after operations were moved to Fowey. NICHOLAS LEACH

The lifeboat house of 1869 at Port Mellon, now today converted into a private house. NICHOLAS LEACH

where obtaining a crew was easier. The boathouse subsequently became the Lifeboat Cafe and a beach shop with the old service boards on display inside.

MEVAGISSEY. Mevagissey lifeboat station was established in 1869 by the RNLI. The lifeboat was initially kept at the neighbouring village of Port Mellon, where a small cove with a relatively well sheltered beach afforded a good launch site from the lifeboat house built there. This house, used until 1888, has since been converted into a private residence and is situated at the head of a small slipway made up of rails which run from the road down to the beach.

The station was moved in 1888 to Mevagissey Harbour where the lifeboat was at first kept afloat. However, this arrangement proved unsatisfactory as the lifeboat sustained some damage while on moorings and so, in 1895-6, a new concrete lifeboat house with a slipway was built in the outer harbour. A new, improved lifeboat, named *James Chisholm* (ON.403), was also supplied. When a motor lifeboat was sent to the neighbouring Fowey station in 1928, the

lifeboat was withdrawn from Mevagissey and the station was closed in 1930. The house built in the outer harbour is still standing, little altered externally, in use as a Marine Aquarium, with the slipway still intact.

PORTLOE. The short-lived lifeboat station at Portloe, founded in 1870 and closed in 1887, was intended to provide cover between Falmouth and Mevagissey but its lifeboat never performed a single rescue. In spite of this short life, two lifeboat houses were built, the first in 1870 when the station opened. This house, built at right angles opposite where the road goes down to the sea, proved unsatisfactory due to the difficulty in getting the lifeboat onto the beach for launching. It has since become an Anglican Church and stands on the landward side of the road through the village, above the steep slope down to the beach. In 1877, a second boathouse was built at the head of the small beach. This was used until the station was closed in 1887 after the RNLI had realised that getting the lifeboat out of the cove in bad weather was too difficult and opportunities for it to perform any rescue

The lifeboat house in Mevagissey's outer harbour built in 1895-6, now an aquarium. NICHOLAS LEACH

The lifeboat house at Portloe built in 1877 and now a private residence. NICHOLAS LEACH

Falmouth's 17m Severn lifeboat RICHARD COX SCOTT (ON.1256) at Pendennis Walk. NICHOLAS LEACH

work were limited. The 1877 house later became a school room and is now a private residence.

FALMOUTH. The Falmouth lifeboat station was established in 1867 and a lifeboat house built near the Dry Docks. The first lifeboats performed very few rescues, and it was not until the 1890s that the services of Falmouth lifeboat were called upon with any frequency. In 1918 the lifeboat was moved to a mooring in the middle of the port's large natural harbour. In 1931 the first motor lifeboat, the former Penlee lifeboat *The Brothers* (ON.671), a 45ft Watson built in 1922, was placed on station.

Since the 1970s, the station has operated 'fast' all-weather lifeboats and was served for almost twenty years by the 52ft Arun *Elizabeth Ann* (ON.1058). In 1980, a rigid-

hulled inshore lifeboat, also kept afloat, was placed on service until being replaced in 1987 by a rigid-inflatable Atlantic 21. In 1993, a new berth with pontoon boarding facilities was constructed close to a purpose-built ILB house for the Atlantic 21, which was launched from a trolley, at Tinners Walk, Port Pendennis. This building is shared with the Coastguard and the station's service boards are displayed on the wall of an adjacent building. In May 2002, the station's new 17m Severn *Richard Cox Scott* (ON.1256) was named by HM The Queen at the beginning of the monarch s Golden Jubilee tour.

PORTHOUSTOCK. The lifeboat station at Porthoustock was established in 1869 and a lifeboat house was built at the head of the beach. The most notable rescue that the Porthoustock lifeboat was involved in

The ILB house and crew facility at Falmouth with 17m Severn at moorings on the left and the ramp down which the ILB is launched on the right. NICHOLAS LEACH

The lifeboat house at Porthoustock built in 1869 and used until the station closed in 1942. NICHOLAS LEACH

THE MODERN LIFEBOAT FLEET

The RNLI currently operates four different types of all-weather lifeboat, all of which are in service at stations in Cornwall. In addition, Atlantic 75 rigid-inflatable and D class inflatable inshore lifeboats are in service.

Severn
*17m x 5.5m,
speed 25 knots, afloat*

Trent
*14m x 4.53m,
speed 25 knots, afloat*

Tyne
*47ft x 15ft,
speed 17 knots, slipway*

Mersey
*12m x 3.8m,
speed 16 knots, carriage*

The lifeboat house at Coverack built in 1901, used throughout the life of the station and now the Lifeboat Café. NICHOLAS LEACH

occurred on the evening of 14 October 1898 when the steamship *Mohegan*, sailing to New York, struck the Manacle Rocks. The ship immediately began sinking, but despite four lifeboats being on the scene none could find the wreck in the darkness. However, the Porthoustock lifeboat was launched and under Coxswain James Hill managed to save 44 of the 51 survivors; sadly over 100 people were not saved. The station was closed in 1942 but the house remains unaltered on the landward side of the road through the village. It is now used as the Village Hall, and inside are displayed the station's service boards.

COVERACK. The station at Coverack was opened in 1901 to improve lifeboat coverage of the Manacles following the *Mohegan* disaster. A lifeboat house and slipway were built at the harbour for the station's first lifeboat, a sailing Watson type named *Constance Melanie* (ON.458). The 35ft 6in Liverpool motor *The Three Sisters* (ON.771), was sent to the station in 1934. After twenty years she was replaced by a larger motor lifeboat, *William Taylor of Oldham* (ON.907), the first lifeboat to be fitted with commercial diesel engines. This lifeboat was withdrawn in May 1972 to be replaced by an inflatable inshore lifeboat operational during the summer months. The ILB was withdrawn in October 1978 as the area was deemed to be effectively covered by the new Falmouth all-weather lifeboat, and the station was closed. The lifeboat house built in 1901, used throughout the operational life of the station, has since been converted into the Lifeboat Café with service boards displayed outside.

CADGWITH. The Cadgwith lifeboat station was established in 1867 to cover the eastern side of the Lizard peninsula. The lifeboat house built in 1867 was used throughout the life of

The lifeboat house at the small village of Cadgwith built in 1867 facing the beach is now used by the local Pilot Gig Club. NICHOLAS LEACH

Launch of Frederick H. Pilley (ON.657) at Lizard, where she served from 1920 to 1934. From an old postcard in the author's collection

The old lifeboat house at Church Cove used for the Lizard No.2 lifeboat. Nicholas Leach

the station. All of the lifeboats, including the motor lifeboat which was sent to the station in 1941, were launched across the beach using manpower. The station was closed in 1963 once the new station at Kilcobben Cove had become fully operational. The boathouse became a store, and is now used by the Cadgwith Pilot Gig Club for storage of their gig. On the walls of the building are pictures and other items relating to the lifeboat station.

THE LIZARD. The lifeboat station at The Lizard has a somewhat complicated history. The first Lizard station was established by the RNLI at Polpeor Cove following the wreck of the steamship *Czar* in January 1859. The steamer's crew were rescued by local boatmen, drawing attention to the need for a lifeboat in the area. The RNLI then set about establishing a station in 1859 and a boathouse was built near the top of the

roadway leading down into Polpeor Cove. This house was used until a new house was built in 1892 nearer to the launching area on an adjacent site. This second house was used until 1914/15. It was then converted into a winch-house as a new lifeboat house with a deep-water slipway was built for the station's first motor lifeboat. This was used until 1961, being replaced by the Kilcobben station. Both of these boathouses are still standing, and were in a rather poor condition until being renovated in the early years of the twenty-first century.

In 1885 a No.2 station was established at Church Cove, where a lifeboat house built, but remained operational only until 1899. The house was at an angle facing away from the sea, so launching the boat was a complicated procedure. It had to be turned through a sharp right turn before plunging over the skids into the water. The house has been little altered externally, and both

The old lifeboat houses at Lizard Point, the most southerly point of the British Isles. Nicholas Leach

The first Mullion lifeboat, DANIEL J. DRAPER, outside the lifeboat house. The station was operational from 1867 to 1908. RNLI

enamel roundels can be seen either side of the main door, over which the stone plaque commemorating the donor also remains. It was used as a store then later converted into a private residence.

In 1961, a new lifeboat house with a roller slipway was built at Kilcobben Cove, between the villages of Lizard and Cadgwith, for the 52ft Barnett lifeboat *The Duke of Cornwall (Civil Service No.33)*. The new station replaced that at Lizard Point and eventually that at Cadgwith as well. From 1961 until 1987, it was known as Lizard-Cadgwith, and from 1987 as The Lizard. The house was modified in 1988 to take a new 47ft Tyne fast slipway lifeboat.

The lifeboat house at Porthleven built in 1893/4. The original slipway used for launching is now demolished. NICHOLAS LEACH

MULLION. The lifeboat station at Mullion was established by the RNLI in 1867 to give additional protection to the coast between Porthleven and the Lizard. It was closed in 1908 after conditions in the locality had changed rendering the station no longer necessary. The lifeboat house built in 1867, used throughout the life of the station, has been demolished although the original barometer can still be seen displayed in Mullion village.

PORTHLEVEN. The station at Porthleven was established in 1863 and a lifeboat house was built at Breageside. Because of difficulties in launching the lifeboat from a carriage, a new boathouse with a slipway was built in 1893/4 on the west side of the entrance channel to the harbour. The station was closed in 1929 as the motor lifeboats at Penlee and the Lizard could adequately cover the area. Since then the launching slipway has been destroyed, but the house itself became a store and was later converted into a small museum known as The Shipwreck Centre.

MARAZION. An inshore lifeboat station was established in 1990 for a trial period with a relief D class inflatable. The trials proved successful, and the station was confirmed as fully operational in 1991. The ILB was kept in one of the quayside buildings on St Michael's

Relief D class ILB inside the small Marazion boathouse on St Michael's Mount. NICHOLAS LEACH

The lifeboat house at Penzance built in 1884 at the foot of Jennings Street and little altered since operations ceased. NICHOLAS LEACH

Mount, and launched into the small harbour beneath the Mount, which faces the village of Marazion. However, the station was closed and the lifeboat withdrawn on 31 October 2001 following extensive evaluation of services in the area by the RNLI with an Atlantic ILB operating from nearby Newlyn Harbour. Problems with manning the boat had arisen as insufficient crew were available during the winter months when only three helmsmen were on call. In the summer, when many students work on the Mount, obtaining a crew was not a problem. But an examination of operational cover during an 18-month study in the Mounts Bay area showed that an Atlantic 75 stationed at Newlyn, together with the Penlee all-weather lifeboat, could provide the required operational cover in the Marazion area. During the station's operational life from in 1990 to 2001, its lifeboats and crews launched 112 times on service and saved twenty-one lives.

PENZANCE. The early history of the station at Penzance is described in the first section of the book. Suffice to say, a lifeboat was first placed here in 1803, but failed to fulfil its purpose due to lack of funds. Despite several further attempts to establish a station, only in 1853 when full control was passed to the RNLI, was effective rescue provision available.

The station was located in various different parts of the port, but from 1884 until 1917, when the station was closed, the boat was kept in a lifeboat house built at the foot of Jennings Street. Once the station at Penlee Point to the south of Penzance was fully operational, and the area was then adequately covered, the lifeboat was removed. The boathouse of 1884 remains standing and was used a display centre for the local Branch of the RNLI.

NEWLYN AND PENLEE. In 1908, the Penzance lifeboat was transferred to Newlyn harbour where she was kept until 1913. No boathouse was built as the lifeboat was kept under a tarpaulin on her carriage at the water's edge, ready for launching. This boat was moved again in 1913 to the new lifeboat house and slipway built at Penlee Point, to the north of Mousehole, which enabled a

Penlee's Atlantic 75 inshore lifeboat PAUL ALEXANDER (B-787) outside the ILB house at Newlyn being washed down after exercise. NICHOLAS LEACH

The moorings in Newlyn Harbour for Penlee's 17m Severn lifeboat IVAN ELLAN (ON.1265). NICHOLAS LEACH

quick launch to be effected. This house, situated on the road from Penzance to Mousehole, was used for the Penlee station until 1983 and has since been maintained by the RNLI, occasionally housing relief lifeboats.

When a new 52ft Arun fast afloat lifeboat was allocated to Penlee following the 1981 disaster, it had to be kept at moorings so an afloat berth was dredged in Newlyn Harbour and crew facilities were constructed on the adjacent quayside. In 2002, a new pontoon and walkway were installed to provide a new berth for the 17m Severn lifeboat and improve boarding arrangements for the crew. In 2001, an inshore lifeboat station was established following the closure of the nearby Marazion station at St Michael's Mount. An ILB house was constructed to house the Atlantic 75 and its launching rig. In 2003 a new boarding pontoon was installed in Newlyn Harbour

The lifeboat house at Penlee Point is now empty but still maintained in full order by the RNLI with the memorial garden adjacent. NICHOLAS LEACH

Penlee lifeboats IVAN ELLEN (ON.1265) and Atlantic 75 B-787 PAUL ALEXANDER on exercise together in Mount's Bay. NICHOLAS LEACH

The lifeboat house at St Agnes (Isles of Scilly) looking up the two slipways. NICHOLAS LEACH

The St Mary's lifeboat house of 1874 on the beach at Portcressa. NICHOLAS LEACH

ST AGNES (Isles of Scilly). St Agnes was the second station to be established on the Isles of Scilly when it was opened in 1890. A lifeboat house was built at Priglis Bay in 1890 for a carriage launched lifeboat. However, difficulties in launching were experienced, and so in 1903 two long stone slipways were built to improve matters. These were 1068ft long in total; one was used for launching at high-water and the longer one for low water launching. The lifeboat was mounted on a trolley which ran on rails down to the water. The station was closed in 1920 after a motor lifeboat had been placed at neighbouring St Mary's. The lifeboat house built in 1890 is now used as a store and the remains of the two slipways can still be seen.

ST MARY'S (Isles of Scilly).
The first two lifeboats at St Mary's were funded by the RNIPLS and have been described in the main body of the text. The first came in 1837 and the second in 1840,

but neither was a success and in 1855 the station was closed when the lifeboat was found to be in a poor condition. It was reopened by the RNLI in 1874 following two major shipwrecks in the area and a lifeboat house was built on the beach at Porthcressa. The first lifeboat, a 37ft twelve-oared self-righter named *Henry Dundas*, was launched from a carriage over the beach.

The house at Porthcressa was used until 1899 when it was replaced by a larger house with a roller slipway at Carn Thomas, on the east side of the harbour, which enabled a much speedier launch. This house was largely rebuilt in 1914 to accommodate a new motor lifeboat, *Elsie* (ON.648), which arrived in October 1919. It remained in use until 1981, adapted and enlarged for subsequent motor lifeboats. Then, when the lifeboat was placed afloat at moorings in the middle of the harbour, it was converted to take the boarding boat as well as provide adequate crew facilities.

The scene at St Mary's during the naming ceremony of the station's current lifeboat. PHIL WEEKS

The lifeboat house and slipway at Porthcressa, St Mary's, is now used to house the station's boarding boat. NICHOLAS LEACH

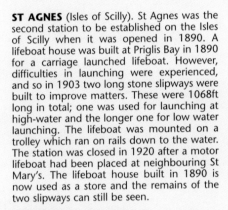

47ft Tyne NORMAN SALVESEN (ON.1121) leaving Sennen Cove where she has been stationed since December 1998. TIM STEVENS

SENNEN COVE. The lifeboat station at Sennen Cove was established in 1853 when a small six-oared self-righter was supplied and a boathouse was built at the expense of the Lord of the Manor. A new lifeboat house was built in 1876 on the landward-side of the Cove and this was used until 1896 for the lifeboats which were carriage launched. It has since been converted into a general store with a heavily disguised frontage.

In 1896, another lifeboat house was completed on the site of the boathouse built in 1864. This house remains in use but has been extensively altered and enlarged since its original construction. The first major alterations took place in 1919 when a new slipway was provided for the station's first motor lifeboat with a turntable inside the house so the boat could be recovered bow first and then turned to face seawards once rehoused.

Further alterations in 1927-29 saw the construction of two slipways to provide a unique launch and recovery system. Originally the boat would be recovered up one slipway bow first, then turned inside the house on a turntable ready for the next launch. This system has since been abandoned and the lifeboat is now recovered stern first.

In 1994, the station was upgraded when an inshore lifeboat became operational. The ILB was kept in the boathouse. To launch, it was craned onto the slipway and, on a trolley, lowered down into the water.

In 1997-98, the boathouse and slipway were adapted for the 47ft Tyne class lifeboat and a new launch slip was created down the long slipway to make launching the ILB easier at low water. In 2000-01, a new roof was

The lifeboat house and slipway as rebuilt and enlarged in 1927-29 and again in 2000-01 with the shallow-arched steel roof. NICHOLAS LEACH

The lifeboat house in Fore Stree, St Ives, built in 1867 as it is today. NICHOLAS LEACH

The 1993-4 lifeboat house on the West Pier at St Ives for 12m Mersey class lifeboat. NICHOLAS LEACH

The St Agnes inshore lifeboat house at Trevaunance Cove with the tractor house to the left and D class to the right. NICHOLAS LEACH

built for the lifeboat house as part of extensive rebuilding work so that a new 16m Tamar class slipway lifeboat could be accommodated. The existing gable-ended roof was removed to be replaced by a shallow-arched steel structure. Internally, the new three-storey accommodation incorporated a ground floor ILB changing room, first floor ALB changing room, and a crew room on the second floor. The refurbished lifeboat house was formally opened on 16 February 2001 by the former Divisional Inspector for the South West, George Rawlinson.

In November 2004, an announcement was made that Sennen Cove will be allocated a new Tamar class lifeboat within the next three years which will be provided through a fund-raising appeal by the City of London Branch of the RNLI. The Branch intends to raise £1 million as part of the celebrations to commemorate the 200th Anniversary of the Battle of Trafalgar. The fund-raising activities set in motion by the City of London included an auction of Faberge Eggs which helped to boost local fund-raising activities. The new lifeboat will be named *City of London III*.

ST IVES. The first St Ives lifeboat was built in 1840 and operated by a local committee. It was not operational by 1860 and in 1861 the RNLI opened their own station here. A lifeboat house near the Island was built, but was only used until 1867 as launching the lifeboat from it proved difficult. This first boathouse, located near Porthgwidden Beach, is now used as a store. A new house was built in 1867 in Fore Street, which was altered and modified a number of times as the harbour developed. It was rebuilt on its present site in 1911 on the Quay and housed the lifeboats until 1993.

As this house was too small for the 12m Mersey class lifeboat being built for the station, a new purpose-built lifeboat house was constructed in 1993-4 at the West Pier, and finished in natural granite to fit in with its surroundings. This building houses both all weather and inshore lifeboats, as well as their respective launching vehicles. A launching slipway into the harbour was also constructed.

The inshore lifeboat, the first of which was sent to St Ives in 1964, was kept in a small house at the Sloop Car Park, off Fish Hill, until 1993. It was then co-located with the all-weather lifeboat in the West Pier boathouse. A memorial to those lost in the 1939 disaster was set into the front wall of the 1911 boathouse and was incorporated into the front wall of the new boathouse where it can now be seen.

HAYLE. The RNLI established a lifeboat station at Hayle in 1866 and three lifeboats served the station during its half century existence. A lifeboat house was built in 1897 and used until the station was closed in 1920 as a result of the decline in the port's coastal trade. The house was relocated on the quay next to the river, and used as a store by the local power station until being dismantled during the 1980s.

ST AGNES. An ILB station was established in 1968 and is located at Trevaunance Cove, St Agnes. The ILB is kept in a small house on the road leading to the beach, and launched using a small tractor. In 2004 a new crew building, situated at the top of the hill leading down to the Cove, was provided by converting a house that was purchased and renovated over three months. The building improved shore facilities for the station's

The lifeboat house on Towan Head at Newquay built in 1899 opposite one of the steepest slipways in the country. NICHOLAS LEACH

Launch of Newquay's D class inflatable D-636 VALERIE WILSON in the harbour at the end of her naming ceremony in May 2005. PAUL RICHARDS

volunteers as well as an outlet for the local fund-raising branch.

NEWQUAY. The Newquay lifeboat station was established in 1860. The first lifeboat was kept in a boathouse on Fore Street, in the middle of the town, and taken down to the beach by carriage. This original lifeboat house built in 1860 is now used as a shop.

In 1899 a new lifeboat house was built on Towan Head and a slipway directly into the sea was also built. The slipway, with a gradient of 1:2.5, was one of the steepest in the country. Both house and slipway remain largely unaltered; the house is used by the local council, and has a plaque identifying its original use above the main door. In 1934 the station was closed but was reopened in 1940 as a temporary wartime measure. When the war ended in 1945, the station was again closed.

The inshore lifeboat was opened in 1965 and an ILB house was built in the harbour. In 1994, the station was upgraded and a new double ILB house was built on the same site to accommodate two inshore lifeboats: an Atlantic 75 rigid-inflatable and D class inflatable.

PADSTOW. The station at Padstow was established in 1827 and operated by the Padstow Harbour Association, described

above. The first lifeboat house, built by the Padstow Harbour Association at Hawker's Cove, possibly in 1829, is still standing and has living accommodation above. In 1856 the RNLI took the station over and continued operating from Hawker's Cove. The first RNLI boathouse was built alongside the Harbour Association house, but all that now remains is part of the left hand wall, the concrete base and the keelway and launchway.

Most unusually, a small house was built in Trethillick Lane in 1883 for the station in which a launching carriage was kept. This would be used to take the lifeboat to a beach further afield, such as Harlyn Bay, if it was too rough for the lifeboat to cross the Bar. If a launch elsewhere was needed, the Coastguards would alert the local farmers who would attach the horses to the carriage and then bring it round to the harbour. Here it would meet the lifeboat which had been launched from Hawker's Cove and rowed round in the river. The lifeboat would then be pulled onto the carriage and taken to a site from where a successful launch could be accomplished. This small carriage house is still standing on the high ground about half a mile to the west of the town, now used as a farm store.

The first lifeboat to be kept at moorings in the estuary was the ill-fated steam lifeboat

The small house in Trethillick Lane, about half a mile out of Padstow, used for housing the lifeboat's carriage. NICHOLAS LEACH

The winch house on the cliffs at Trevose Head above the Padstow lifeboat house built facing Mother Ivey's Bay in 1967. NICHOLAS LEACH

Looking up the slipway to the lifeboat house built at Hawker's Cove in 1931 for the Padstow No.2 lifeboats. The 35ft 6in motor self-righter JOHN AND SARAH ELIZA STYCH (ON.743) is in the boathouse.
COURTESY OF JOHN CORIN

which arrived in 1899. Between 1901 and 1929 a steam tug and lifeboat were operated from moorings with considerable success. In 1929 when a motor lifeboat was sent to the station, it was kept at moorings in the estuary. In 1931 a second smaller motor lifeboat was sent to the station, and a new house with roller slipway was built at Hawker's Cove for this boat which became the No.2 lifeboat. This house was used until 1962 by when the silting of the estuary prevented an efficient launch at all states of the tide. It was unused and empty for a number of years, with the original blue enamel facia boards over the doors and the original winch inside. More recently it has been converted into a private residence. The station was moved from the estuary in 1967 and a new boathouse and slipway built at Trevose Head, already described in the main body of the text.

Two memorials to those lost in the 1900 disaster can be seen: one in Padstow Cemetery to seven of the men and another in St Merryn's Churchyard to the eighth man.

The lifeboat house and slipway at Trevose Head with 47ft Tyne JAMES BURROUGH (ON.1094) inside. Piling for the new boathouse under construction can be seen on the far side of the slipway
NICHOLAS LEACH

In January 2005, plans were announced for a new £5.5 million lifeboat house and slipway to be built alongside the existing boathouse at Trevose Head. The new building will be home to a new 16m Tamar lifeboat due on station in 2006. Work began in April 2005 with most materials brought to the site by sea to reduce road traffic. The unique building has a distinctive shape which it is hoped will rest well against the imposing cliffs at Trevose Head. The existing boathouse remained fully operational throughout the period of the building work.

ROCK An ILB station was established at Rock in March 1994 to cover the Camel river, estuary and bar. The D class inflatable was housed in temporary buildings while the station was being evaluated. Once the evaluation has proved the need for the ILB, a new boathouse was built on the beach in 1997 for ILB and quadbike.

PORT ISAAC. The lifeboat station was established in 1869 by the RNLI. The original lifeboat house, built when the station was opened, was situated on the hill leading down to the east side of the small bay as this was the only site available at the time. Launching the boat involved taking it down a steep slope on the carriage, through the narrow streets and onto the beach. Rehousing required a considerable effort as

Rock's D class inflatable D-634 RUSPER is taken afloat in the Camel estuary at the end of her naming ceremony in April 2005. PAUL RICHARDS

The lifeboat house at Port Isaac built in 1927 and used for the ILB since 1993. NICHOLAS LEACH

The original inshore lifeboat house on the South Pier of the locks at Bude, used for the D class inflatable until 2002. NICHOLAS LEACH

the boat had to be hauled back up the hill to the house.

This house was used until 1927, later became the local Post Office and is now a souvenir shop. In 1927, a new lifeboat house was built more conveniently located at the head of the beach and used until the station closed in 1933. It then became a garage for the Slipway House Hotel. In 1967 the station was reopened by the RNLI with a inshore lifeboat, which was kept for more than twenty years in a building on the beach used by Port Isaac Fishermen Ltd. In 1993 the RNLI re-acquired the boathouse built in 1927 and converted it to house the ILB.

In May 1997, a new D class inflatable was placed on station, D-517, funded by the Officers and Soldiers of the Royal Logistics Corp with contributions from other regiments and named *Spirit of the PCS RE.* However, this boat was capsized and wrecked on service to two people stranded on a beach on 7 September 1998. Fortunately all of the stranded people, including the ILB's crew, were saved but the ILB itself was a total loss. The station s old ILB, D-366, which had

The impressive inshore lifeboat house built in 2002 on Bude's Summerleaze Beach for the station's D class inflatable and launching tractor. NICHOLAS LEACH

served from 1988 to 1997, was returned to the station as a temporary replacement until, in 1999, a new ILB funded by a local appeal was provided to replace the boat that had been wrecked.

BUDE. The history of the Bude lifeboat station is not particularly well documented until the RNLI took over its running in 1853 and supplied a new lifeboat. In 1863 a new lifeboat house was built at the side of the canal, into which the boat could be launched if necessary. This house was used until 1922 when the station closed after a large motor lifeboat had entered service at Padstow to the south to cover the area. The house has been much altered internally and is now used as holiday flats; the donor memorial stone over the doorway is still visible.

In 1966 the station was reopened by the RNLI with a D class inflatable. The ILB was kept in a small house on the South Pier by the lock, and launched from a trolley over the large beach. However, the original facilities proved to be inadequate for the needs of the twenty-first century, and so a new lifeboat house was constructed in 2001-2 at Summerleaze beach. The impressive new building, built at a cost of approximately £490,000 by E. Thomas Construction, the South West building operation of John Mowlem & Co, provides a boatroom to house the D class inflatable, its carriage and launching vehicle. Supporting facilities include a workshop and storage for fuel, with a crew/training room for regular exercise and instruction sessions. The building was designed to fit in with its site and surroundings, and was constructed from high quality materials to resist the maritime conditions and enhance the coastal scene. The new station has become a focal point at the entrance to the beach and an ideal base for the local volunteers.

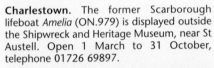

37ft Oakley Amelia (ON.979) on display outside the Shipwreck & Heritage Museum at Charlestown. Nicholas Leach

The former Looe lifeboat Ryder (ON.489) now restored and pictured under oars. Paul Richards

Charlestown. The former Scarborough lifeboat *Amelia* (ON.979) is displayed outside the Shipwreck and Heritage Museum, near St Austell. Open 1 March to 31 October, telephone 01726 69897.

Fowey. Since 2002, a gathering of historic lifeboats has been organised over one weekend during the summer. The lifeboats moor at a pontoon and are often open to the public. A parade of sail also usually takes place.

Land's End. The lifeboat *James and Catherine MacFarlane*, which served at Padstow and the Lizard, is on display outside the Land's End complex. This has various exhibitions including one on Air Sea Rescue. Tel 0870 458 0099.

Polperro. The former Looe lifeboat *Ryder* (ON.489), built in 1902, has been fully restored and moored in the harbour close to the Polperro Heritage Museum of Smuggling and Fishing. Tel 01503 272423.

St Ives. The former St Ives lifeboat *James Stevens No.10* (ON.435) has been extensively restored and, since 2004, employed as a trip boat at her original home port.

Former St Ives lifeboat James Stevens No.10 (ON.435) restored as a trip boat and kept at moorings in the harbour of her original home port. Nicholas Leach

The impressive site of historic lifeboats gathered at Fowey in 2003 for the annual ex lifeboat rally held at the picturesque port every summer. Nicholas Leach

Former Padstow and Lizard lifeboat JAMES AND CATHERINE MACFARLANE (ON.989) at Land's End. NICHOLAS LEACH

FURTHER READING

Allan, David and Smith, Tony, *RNLI St Ives: Past-Present-Future* (1994).
Berry, Claude, *A Century of Service – Story of Padstow's Lifeboats* (1927).
Corin, John and Farr, Grahame, *Penlee Lifeboat* (Penlee & Penzance Branch of the RNLI, 1983).
Cox, Barry (Ed.), *Lifeboat Gallantry* (Spink & Son Ltd, London, 1998).
Farr, Grahame, *Papers on Life-boat History, No.5: The Steam Life-boats 1889-1928* (Bristol, 1981).
Kittridge, Alan, *Cornwall's Maritime Heritage* (Twelveheads Press, Truro, 2nd edition, 2003)
Leach, Nicholas, *The Origins of the Lifeboat Service* (1992).
Leach, Nicholas, *Fowey Lifeboats* (Tempus Publishing Ltd. 2002).
Leach, Nicholas, *Sennen Cove Lifeboats - 150 years of life-saving* (Tempus Publishing Ltd, 2003).
Morris, Jeff, *The Story of the Isles of Scilly Lifeboats* (1987).
Noall, Cyril, *Cornwall's Early Lifeboats 1803-1939* (Tor Mark Press, Penryn, 1989).
Noall, Cyril and Farr, Grahame, *Wreck and Rescue round the Cornish Coast I: The story of the North Coast Lifeboats* (D Bradford Barton Ltd, Truro, 1964).
Noall, Cyril and Farr, Grahame, *Wreck and Rescue round the Cornish Coast II: The story of the Land's End Lifeboats* (D. Bradford Barton Ltd, Truro, 1965).
Noall, Cyril and Farr, Grahame, *Wreck and Rescue round the Cornish Coast III: The story of the South Coast Lifeboats* (D. Bradford Barton Ltd, Truro, 1965).
Phillips, George C, *A Short History of the Padstow Lifeboat* (1995).
Warner, Oliver, *The Lifeboat Service: A History of the RNLI 1824-1974* (Cassell, London, 1974).

ACKNOWLEDGMENTS
I am very grateful to successive members of staff at RNLI Headquarters in Poole for providing me with research facilities over many years; to the late Grahame Farr, whose records held by the RNLI have been of considerable help while preparing this book; to the coxswains, crews and personnel at the lifeboat stations in Cornwall, who were helpful, hospitable and generous of their time during my visits to the county and enabled me to take many of the photos included in the book; to Paul Richards of Fowey and Tim Stevens of Sennen Cove for supplying a steady stream of excellent photos; and finally to Sarah for her support, constructive comments and companionship during our many visits to Cornwall over the past decade.
Nicholas Leach, Birmingham, December 2005